THE POPULATION EXPLOSION

a liberal studies book

IN THE SAME SERIES

COVER: This poor little fellow could be Abiola from West Africa, Suffri from India, Ahmed from Pakistan . . . or any child from one of the underdeveloped countries. In fact he represents every other child in the world, and this book is concerned with his plight.

C. W. Park

THE POPULATION EXPLOSION

a liberal studies book

HEINEMANN EDUCATIONAL BOOKS
LONDON

HEINEMANN EDUCATIONAL BOOKS LTD

LONDON EDINBURGH MELBOURNE AUCKLAND
TORONTO SINGAPORE HONG KONG KUALA LUMPUR
IBADAN NAIROBI JOHANNESBURG
LUSAKA NEW DELHI

ISBN 0 435 46532 5

© C. W. Park 1965
First published 1965
Reprinted 1966, 1969, 1970, 1971, 1975

Published by Heinemann Educational Books Ltd
48 Charles Street, London W1X 8AH
Printed Offset Litho in Great Britain by
Cox & Wyman Ltd, London, Fakenham and Reading

FOR CHRISTOPHER

in the hope that he may see
the world of A.D. 2000 free from
the pressures of
population, poverty, power politics, and pessimism.

ACKNOWLEDGEMENTS

The author and publishers wish to thank His Royal Highness, Prince Philip, Duke of Edinburgh, for permission to quote, by way of introduction, parts of His Royal Highness's speech at Church House, Westminster, in November 1964.

Thanks are due also to Professor Ritchie Calder and the *Sunday Times* for permission to reproduce the introduction to Chapter 5 and the diagram on page 52 from the issue of 17th March, 1963; to the Oxford Committee For Famine Relief for supplying the cover photograph; to the United Nations Food and Agriculture Organization for the liberal use of many statistical tables and to the various authors and publishers, quoted in footnotes, to whom references have been made.

CONTENTS

LIST OF DIAGRAMS AND TABLES

INTRODUCTION

'I suppose one could argue that as starvation has always controlled population there is nothing to worry about. Just let nature take its course. I don't believe any decent human being, least of all a Christian, could possibly accept this argument. No matter how hopeless it may seem, we can't give up without a struggle.

'We make so many wild claims for ourselves as human beings. The least we can do is to prove our superior intelligence by controlling our numbers and standard of existence deliberately and willingly.

'We know Nature's solution and I can't help feeling that we ought to try to do better than that. Make no mistake, for the first time in man's history we have the power to control our environment and our numbers deliberately. Nature may still have surprises in store for us, but, by and large, if the world runs into a disaster we have only ourselves to blame. We could have prevented it . . .

'Somehow or other this great struggling, squabbling mass has got to come to realize the gravity of the situation which is confronting it. And it has got to generate the will to do something about it.'

HIS ROYAL HIGHNESS, PRINCE PHILIP
DUKE OF EDINBURGH

1: THE GREATEST REVOLUTION?

The demographers estimate that in little over a generation, in the year A.D. 2000, the population of the world will double approximately from its present 3,300 millions* to well over 6,000 millions.

The Problem. This is a staggering prediction. From time to time voices are raised in screeching alarm that mankind is heading for disaster; that we cannot feed such a hugely increased population; that we are heading towards a world-wide cataclysm of starvation, disease and social disintegration. Occasionally our conscience is pricked by appeals for 'Freedom From Hunger' and by photographs of skeletal, rib-caged babies such as the one shown on the cover. But conscience is soon shrugged off by material matters of the moment. We hear that a half of the world's population is underfed and undernourished and we are vaguely impressed. Malnutrition and death, however, are continents away in the semi-deserts, eroded valleys, parched savannahs and impoverished soils of overpopulated lands. People die old in body and experience, yet young in years, in the quiet of their pitiful homes, despite the aid of the United Nations Organization, individual countries and voluntary organizations.

And this is happening today! What, then, is the prospect for the turn of the century when young readers of this book will be only middle-aged? Will this 'Greatest Revolution', in the space of little more than a generation eclipse any other development in the history of man, be it agrarian, industrial or nuclear? The following pages are devoted to considering the extent and likelihood of this increase. The pressure points need examination; the massive side-effects – medical, moral and

**American Bureau of Population Studies Report.* December 1964.

political, require considerable investigation. Possible solutions are posed without which the turn of the century may witness a calamitous deterioration in the social development of mankind.

THE BACKGROUND OF POPULATION INCREASES

It is important to realize that the estimated increase of the next generation will not be typical of man's rate of reproduction over the centuries, otherwise there would be *a million times* the present number of human beings – a figure for which the earth could not provide standing room, let alone foodstuffs. War, disease, famine and the development of new lands and resources have been, in the past, Nature's safety valves. But with man's control of his environment the span of life is increasing and the infant mortality rate is being reduced. More people, living longer, beget more people at an increasingly greater rate.

Man, as a species, is of considerable antiquity. In the absence of reliable evidence we can estimate that, from a primitive state, he is about half a million years old. Recent and projected population increases, therefore, represent only a minute snippet of his history. For tens of thousands of years he remained a nomadic hunter and fruit picker controlled and decimated by his environment. In large or small groups he lived a precarious existence and his history is studded with telltales of famine. The Old Testament supplies liberal evidence; re-read the problems of Joseph in ancient Egypt. In 436 B.C., Romans desperately threw themselves into the Tiber as famine swept the city. The Durga Devi famine in India ended in 1407, having lasted twelve years, and the Bengal famine of 1760 lasted ten years and wiped out a third of the inhabitants. The devastating North China Famine of 1877 took the lives of nearly 10 million peasants and, nearer home, the Irish potato famine of 1846–7 catapulted desperate men across the Atlantic. Even today some 50,000 Indians die of starvation annually. These are but isolated examples of the way in which Nature has kept population increases under control.

The relative slowness of population growth up to the beginning of the nineteenth century was due to two main factors which, in turn, stemmed from the control of the environment already mentioned. Over the whole period birth rates must have been higher than death rates otherwise the human race would have perished. But the slow rate of growth, even allowing for a high birth rate (for which no figures are available) was due to a high rate of infant mortality. Possibly a hundred children in every thousand were lost at birth (in Britain today the infant mortality rate is twenty-six per thousand) and the struggle to survive through infancy was acute. In addition to this, early man's expectation of life beyond the twenties was a forlorn hope; no doubt it was similar to that in Borneo today where life expectancy at birth is twenty-nine years. A graph of population increases for this period would show pronounced irregularities. Plagues and famines would devastate whole areas. For example, the fourteenth-century Black Death overran Asia and Europe and the effects were so severe that more than a century passed before the graph of population increase could resume its normal trend.

Despite all these vicious attacks, there was a slow increase in numbers under the protective cloak of settled agriculture. The progression from hunter to shifting cultivator to settled agriculturalist allowed man to produce a better shelter, to protect himself more adequately from the elements, to develop domestic crafts, to set food aside for times of need. At first every hand was concerned with producing food but soon certain individuals, adept at various non-agricultural skills, became dependent on the food producers. Specialization started, community life began and the added protection encouraged the increase of population. But this was still basically an agricultural economy and even the civilizations of Babylon, Carthage and Rome could hardly afford more than a fifth of their inhabitants for non-agricultural pursuits.

Piecing together the mosaic of recorded history, researchers have tentatively suggested that the world's population increased from some 10 millions in 7000 B.C. to about 200 millions at the birth of Christ. Even with the development of the agricultural revolution in Western Europe through the enclosure movement, the improvement of farm stock and the realization of the need for crop rotation, it took 1,600 years for this figure to double to about 400 millions. And then, in the mid-eighteenth century the Industrial Revolution, particularly in Great Britain, released the brakes. The need for more non-agricultural workers gave added impetus to the agricultural revolution as the demand for food in expanding urban areas increased. The development of machines, the increase in manufactured goods, the application of the newly-found power to transport – all these things extended man's horizon. For the first time he was beginning to be free from the shackles of his immediate environment. He began to exploit the resources of other lands, trade flourished and voyages of discovery unfolded a new and exciting world. Isolation, a positive check to population growth, was being broken down and by about 1830 the world's population was around 1,000 millions.

Fig. 1 indicates the progress of the human snowball. In the beginning the increase was inevitably slow. Whether or not we accept the disputed half a million years as man's time span is of little consequence, for the increase was negligible. It is the nineteenth- and particularly the twentieth-century increases which demand attention. The first 1,000 millions in 1830 ushered in the contestants for the race towards A.D. 2000. By 1850 there was an estimated 1,094 millions and 1900 saw 1,550 millions – a 42 per cent increase. This figure rose to 1,907

Fig. 1. The Human Snowball.

Year	World Population in Millions	Population Increase over Previous Figure	Time required to build up to this Figure
? Half a million years B.C.—Man evolved.			
7000 B.C.	10	—	? ½ million years
Birth of Christ	200	180	7,000 years
A.D. 1600	400	200	1,600 „
1750	700	300	150 „
1830	1,000	300	80 „
1900	1,550	550	70 „
1925	1,907	357	25 „
1950	2,497	590	25 „
1975	3,828	1,331	25 „
2000	6,267	2,439	25 „

Note: Estimates before 1900 are tentative and based on a variety of historical evidence. Twentieth-century estimates and projected population figures (medium assumptions) are from U.N.O. Population Studies No. 28.

millions in 1925 (23 per cent increase) and to nearly 2,500 millions in 1950 (31 per cent increase).

Today the world population is about 3,300 millions and from now until the end of the century we are likely to experience the shock waves of the explosive period.

Fig. 2 graphically illustrates the projected, accumulative effect of the snowball, particularly as the turn of the century is reached. The validity and methods of compilation of future population assumptions are mentioned in Appendix I but, taking 'medium assumptions', i.e. the average of the lowest and highest estimates, the increases are likely to be by 53 per cent from 1950 to 1975 and by 64 per cent in the last quarter of this century. A 'high' assumption gives the increase for

1975 to 2000 as 79 per cent and this could be a more realistic prediction with the passage of time for recent experience has shown that past population predictions are often a cemetery of underestimations.

Fig. 2 illustrates that, whereas it took a hundred years for the second 1,000 millions to develop, the third 1,000 millions was achieved, by about 1960, in thirty years. By 1976, perhaps, another layer of 1,000 millions will have been added to the snowball – a quarter of the total in only sixteen years! The mind boggles at the time taken for each subsequent estimate of 1,000 millions – twelve years and nine years respectively – to give an estimated total world population of 6,000 millions just before the turn of the century.

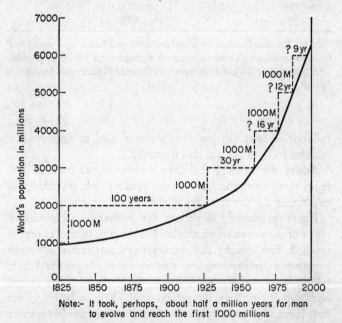

Note:- It took, perhaps, about half a million years for man to evolve and reach the first 1000 millions

Fig. 2. World Population A.D. 1825–2000.

And now the cynic rightly queries, 'How long before we have instant population?' Certainly this rhythm of increase cannot continue and we have evidence that once an industrialized society reaches a high standard of living an automatic population check is released if only to maintain that level. A further danger is that the individual may be submerged beneath the growing masses. To handle two people instead of one, to organize the streamlined specialization required for the effective utilization of resources will demand a high degree of social and political organization together with considerable personal discipline from the individual. Can this be achieved in the jostling rush towards A.D. 2000? If not, the consequent tearing of the social fabric may let slip many of the technological and scientific advances of today. These and other factors, to be considered later, must be borne in mind in considering this precipitous trend in the graph. Undoubtedly a levelling off must occur, but the pertinent question is 'When?'

It may not be beyond the capacity of the earth to carry 6,000 or 7,000 million souls providing time and patience are at hand; but a few decades may be insufficient even with our bounding progress in many fields to cater adequately for a doubled population. Without dabbling in fantasies of planetary migration by A.D. 2000, or allowing for plankton breakfasts cooked in solar-distilled water over atomic power, we must assess the problem of the difficulties of the carrying capacity of the earth in relation to present knowledge and scientific advance. To a consideration of the effects of revolutions in technology, agriculture and communications must be added the 'medical revolution' – the hand which is pushing the snowball. Mortality control and the virtual eradication of epidemics enable us to live, with relative sanity, in congested sanitary cities, But layered living produces massive side-effects of a social nature, only on the fringes of medical control.

Paradoxically, medicine underwrites a large population

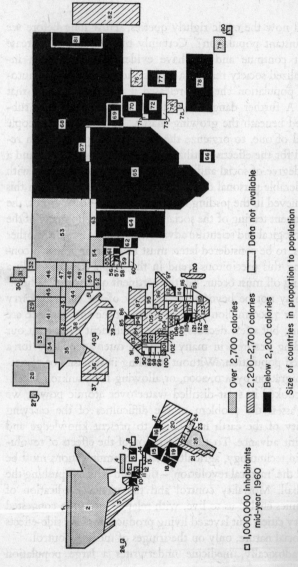

Over 2,700 calories

2,200–2,700 calories

Below 2,200 calories

Data not available

Size of countries in proportion to population

□ 1,000,000 inhabitants mid-year 1960

Fig. 3. The Distorted Shape of a Hungry World.

which, in turn, aggravates the medical problem in endeavouring to underwrite an even larger population . . .

'The question is,' said Humpty Dumpty, 'which is to be master, that's all?'

THE DISTORTED SHAPE OF A HUNGRY WORLD

The statistics quoted so far have been on a world basis and it has been implied that the population explosion is the immediate concern of every human being. No man or nation can stand alone in the world today. The inevitable ripples of individual problems spread far and wide and their influence can be far-reaching.

Just as the habitable areas of the world are unevenly distributed over its surface, so are the people within these areas. This is one of the major problems of the population explosion and before solutions can be considered a comparison of the population densities of the various countries is essential. Fig. 3 illustrates this imbalanced distribution of the world's population today. It is a strange map. The normal confines of geographical boundaries have gone awry because the area scale for each country is based on the size of the population. Compare this with any equal-area world map projection in an atlas. Observe the massive predominance of India and China; Pakistan and Indonesia achieve new significance on this map. These and other areas, shaded black, give cause for grave concern for the inhabitants are likely to be undernourished – a problem which will be discussed in Chapter 5. Notice the increased size of the United Kingdom and Japan, densely populated, industrial regions, compared with the relative insignificance of Canada and Australia.

For the purpose of examining the varying population pressures it is possible to classify the countries of the world into *four* main groups. There are obvious differences, often considerable, within groups and some 'borderline' countries are classified for convenience. Even within a country the population is not evenly spread. In Egypt, for example, the average density is sixty persons per square mile – not a pressing problem statistically; but in reality, the Nile is Egypt and life clings to the water's edge, giving a much higher density in that region. Thus Egypt is classified as a 'high-density' country. India, with an average population density of about 320 per square mile, although classified as a high-density region, may appear to compare favourably with the 1,300 persons per square mile in Barbados but India has tremendous pressure points. On certain teeming, riverine tracts of the Ganges delta estimates of up to 10,000 persons per square mile have been made!

Similarly there are considerable differences in the degree of technological development of countries within these groupings. Occasionally a country's classification, if difficult to define, is quite arbitrary and is based on a regional grouping.

In the following classifications the figure for each country prefers to its position on the map (Fig. 3).

GROUP 1. *Technologically underdeveloped, high density countries* – the crux of the problem – *comprising over half (about 55 per cent) of the world's population*:

4 Cuba, 5 Jamaica, 6 Haiti, 7 Dominican Republic, 8 Puerto Rico, 10 El Salvador, 64 Pakistan, 65 India, 66 Ceylon, 68 China (Mainland), 70 Thailand, 72 Viet Nam, 74 Malaysia, 76 China (Taiwan), 77 Phillipines, 78 Indonesia, 81 Korea, 87 Egypt (U.A.R.), 105 Nigeria.

GROUP 2. *Technologically developed, high-density countries, housing approximately a fifth of the world's population*:

28 United Kingdom, 29 Denmark, 33 Netherlands, 34 Belgium, 35 France, 36 Spain, 37 Portugal, 38 Italy, 39 Sicily, 41 Germany (Fed. Rep.), 42 Switzerland, 43 Austria, 44 Yugoslavia, 45 Germany (East), 46 Poland, 47 Czechoslovakia, 48 Hungary, 49 Rumania, 50 Bulgaria, 52 Greece, 56 Lebanon, 57 Israel, 75 Singapore, 82 Japan.

GROUP 3. *Technologically developed, low-density countries representing about a tenth of the world's population:*

1 Canada, 2 U.S.A., 24 Uruguay, 25 Argentina, 27 Ireland, 30 Norway, 31 Sweden, 32 Finland, 40 Sardinia, 53 U.S.S.R., 79 Australia, 80 New Zealand, 123 South Africa.

GROUP 4. *Technologically underdeveloped, low-density countries often small in size and population. Despite the considerable number and variety they represent only some 15 per cent of the world's population:*

3 Mexico, 9 Guatemala, 11 Honduras, 12 Nicaragua, 13 Costa Rica, 14 Panama, 15 Colombia, 16 Venezuela, 17 Guianas, 18 Ecuador, 19 Peru, 20 Brazil, 21 Chile, 22 Bolivia, 23 Paraguay, 26 Hawaii, 51 Albania, 54 Turkey, 55 Syria, 58 Jordan, 59 Saudi Arabia, 60 Yemen, 61 Iraq, 62 Iran, 63 Afghanistan, 67 Nepal, 69 Burma, 71 Laos, 73 Cambodia, 83 Morocco, 84 Algeria and Sahara, 85 Tunisia, 86 Libya, 88 Mauritania, 89 Gambia, 90 Senegal, 91 Mali, 92 Upper Volta, 93 Niger, 94 Chad, 95 Sudan, 96 Ethiopia, 97 Somalia, 98 Guinea, 99 Sierra Leone, 100 Liberia, 101 Ivory Coast, 102 Ghana, 103 Togo, 104 Dahomey, 106 Cameroun, 107 Central African Republic, 108 Gabon, 109 Congo (Brazzaville), 110 Congo (Leopoldville), 111 Uganda, 112 Kenya, 113 Ruanda-Urundi, 114 Tanzania, 115 Angola, 116 Zambia, 117 S. Rhodesia, 118 Malawi, 119 Mozambique, 120 Madagascar, 121 South West Africa, 122 Bechuanaland, Basutoland, Swaziland.

The countries in Group 1 are the cause of the immediate problem. With the exception of China and Korea, these countries lie in the tropical and sub-tropical zones. Here are found over a half of the world's people, underfed and undernourished, multiplying at a massive rate. Add to this the 15 per cent of the low-density, underdeveloped countries of similar climatic conditions and we are faced with some two-thirds of the world's population at, or below, a basic subsistence level. Groups 2 and 3, the technologically developed countries, lie for the most part in temperate latitudes. And so a basic pattern emerges of heavy population concentrations, with the exception of China, in tropical areas whilst the technologically developed countries of temperate latitudes are less heavily peopled.

What are the reasons for this differential rate of population growth? An understanding of the trend of birth and death rates for these contrasting areas will help clarify the problem.

SOME QUESTIONS

1. Why was the increase in the world's population relatively slow prior to the nineteenth century?

2. Explain the significance of the term 'snowball' in relation to recent world population increases.

3. Consult an equal-area map of the world and compare it with Figure 3. State your conclusions.

DISCUSSION TOPICS

1. Is the increase in world population 'the greatest revolution' that mankind is likely to meet within the next generation?

2. Paradoxically, medicine underwrites a larger population which, in turn, aggravates the medical problem . . . 'The question is,' said Humpty Dumpty, 'which is to be master, that's all?'

2: TWO CHILDREN EVERY SECOND

Birth and death rates are inter-related factors in population growth. They vary considerably according to the economic, social and environmental features of particular regions and countries. The one cancels the other but death does not strike impartially. Industrialized countries have lower death rates than those for underdeveloped, overpopulated countries although medical science is decreasing the death rate in the latter. On the other hand birth rates have decreased in industrialized countries whereas those for the overpopulated regions have tended to remain stable. In considering this relationship the two extremes of man's existence cannot be separated.

The world's birth rate, however, is the factor which usually commands popular attention. We are fed with statistics moulded into emotive language to provide easy assimilation. We are invited, perhaps, to visualize a column of refugees queueing for food (an apt analogy!) increasing by thirty miles in length each day and stretching from Great Britain to New Zealand in a year. The *annual* world increase at present is greater than the population of Great Britain and equal to the estimated British figure for A.D. 2000, i.e. 60 millions. Every *month* 5 million new mouths, equal to half the population of the Greater London Area, cry out for food and comfort. Every *day* the world's population increases by a figure equal to the number of residents in Sunderland or Swansea, Brighton or Carmarthenshire. In ten years, 1951 to 1961, the city of Lincoln increased its population by some 7,000; the human race experiences a similar increase every *hour* of the day and night. And every minute 110 babies gasp their greeting to the world. The clock ticks, the pulse beats; *nearly two children every second!* But these figures quoted on a world basis are unevenly distributed. Political gibes often tack Great Britain on to the U.S.A. as a fifty-first state! This may be just a joke, but it is worth pointing out that between 1940 and 1960 the U.S.A.'s population increase was equivalent to the *total* population of Britain. In the ten years immediately preceding the Second World War, India's population increased by the equivalent of shovelling up all the people of France and deliberately piling them up on areas already heavily overpopulated. One in every four people in the world is Chinese. . . . And so the comparisons continue, but little is said of the world-wide decrease in death rates which allow such arresting statements to be made.

TECHNOLOGICAL BIRTH CONTROL

The massive population increases over the past century have not been caused by any significant increase in the birth rate – an apparent anomaly which is easily resolved by the fact that more and more children have survived birth and early infancy. It is a common misunderstanding to confuse birth rates, usually given as so many per thousand of the population, with total numbers born. It is not incompatible for the startling figures quoted to result, in fact, from a *reduced* birth rate providing there is a corresponding decrease in death rates. Birth rates can fall and yet population can still increase provided women are able to survive the child-bearing years and produce youngsters who, in turn, are able to survive. This is the case in industrialized countries where the birth rate has dropped together with a compensatory reduction in death rates. They have gone, or are going through, a population transition of which that for England and Wales is typical of most of the countries in Group 2 (page 10).

Fig. 4 illustrates this transition and the fact that population

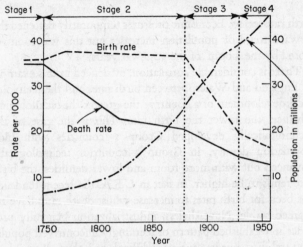

Fig. 4. Population Transition in England and Wales.

can increase coincidentally with falling birth and death rates. The final phase of *Stage 1* is shown. It prevailed throughout the whole span of man's development with high birth rates barely ahead of high death rates. The human race just survived and the increase in population was inevitably slow. *Stage 2* indicates the period between about 1750 and 1880 which was significant for the decline in the death rate as a result of the better living conditions associated with the prosperity of the Industrial Revolution. But birth rates remained fairly high and the 'gap' produced a surge of numbers. This was the beginning of the population explosion for England, gradual at first but with increasing momentum. This upward trend was modified in *Stage 3* as the birth rate sharply declined at a greater rate than that for deaths, the first indication that the limitation of family size was associated not with a high infant mortality rate but with an apparent desire to maintain a higher standard of living. *Stage 4* opened with the depression years of the early thirties. The death rate was levelling off and the birth rate less so. Economic pressures temporarily flattened the upward trend of population increases but this was soon restored by the 'boom' of the post-war years.

There is considerable correlation, evidenced in this example of England and Wales, between birth rates and the technological development of a country; the greater the technological advance, the lower the birth rate. This is the case of the technologically developed Group 2 countries with high population density. In Group 3 countries, technologically advanced but with more room and lower densities, the birth rate tends to be higher. In fact in U.S.A. the recent tendency has been for birth rates to increase whilst death rates have remained stable. Nevertheless, industrialization generally provides an established pattern of seemingly uncontrived population stability, but its causes are difficult to isolate. Certainly it seems to be associated with a desire to maintain and increase a high standard of living. But materialism of this sort is no complete reason for there may be many psychological and social undercurrents. Throughout man's history the odds have been stacked against surviving birth and evading the hazards of infancy and adolescence in order to reach full maturity. Today in industrialized countries 95 per cent of those born enjoy a reasonable span of life. The medical revolution has ensured that these countries only require 'two and a bit' children per family to maintain a relatively stable population. Centuries ago up to ten children per family were often necessary to allow for the caprice of natural selection. Some argue that Nature compensates for dietary deficiency by producing more babies on the principle that the greater the number born, the greater the number who will survive. According to this theory, however, the overpopulation of Group 1 countries results from, and is not the cause of, malnutrition – an interesting suggestion which is difficult to accommodate easily. The arguments are varied but it seems that the full development of an individualistic approach within an educated society results in a voluntary restriction of family size.

Even at this level, however, the birth rate can show slight fluctuations according to the rise and fall of the economic barometer. This happened in the depression years of the 1930s in Britain. The economic doldrums of those pre-war years led to such a decline in the birth rate that immediately after the war a British Royal Commission set out to investigate its causes. Almost at once, it was made redundant by the rush of post-war births. This was construed as a temporary, compensatory bulge resulting from delayed post-war marriages. But the subsequent economic security and affluence have maintained and slightly increased this upward trend. In a modern, industrialized community, therefore, the birth rate seems to be closely tied to material prosperity although the sociological factors cannot be ignored. This tacit acceptance of the limitation of family size has averted an economic and social catastrophe in Europe where birth rates of below 20 per 1,000 are found in such countries as the United Kingdom, France, West Germany, Italy and Switzerland. The fact that they are proceeding at approximately the same pace is unlikely to result in a new cry for *Lebensraum* in Europe (such a cry is more likely to be heard in the Far East). It is to be hoped that they will be concerned more with the need to preserve human dignity – particularly against the squalor which old age often brings. Their problem, perhaps, is not that they will be unable to cope with the present rate of population growth but that they must discover how to solve the social enigmas associated with the sprawl of urban development.

DEATH CONTROL

Fig. 4 illustrates the hand-in-hand progress of the Industrial Revolution and the decline in death rates in England and

Wales, harassed initially by the unhealthy working conditions in factories but generally resulting from a better standard of living and, later, from the benefits of new developments in medicine. Prior to this, disease was rife all over the world. In the 'bloody' Battle of Gettysburg, for example, the mortality rate of the armies of the United States during the first year of the rebellion was 67·6 per thousand of whom only 17·2 per thousand died from wounds and injuries of every kind; disease accounted for 50·4 per thousand. A hundred years ago, of 3,547 deaths in *one week* in a number of British cities, no fewer than 458 were caused by diseases which have been banished, or almost so, in our time by the progress of medicine. Of those 458, 160 resulted from scarlet fever, 76 from enteric fever, 70 from measles, 65 from diarrhoea, 47 from whooping cough, 34 from diphtheria and 4 from small-pox. Indeed, the last century has seen medicine taking an ever-increasing control of the death rate in all industrialized countries.

The arch-enemy, bacteria, was brought under control. The disposal of sewage was organized with a newly found concern for public health and the drinking water of the growing urban communities of industrialized countries was made safe by filtration and chlorination techniques. The effect of the introduction of antibiotics in the 1940s is seen in the reduced death rate for Canadian women in childbirth:* 1930–32, one maternal death per 200 live births; 1940–42, about one in 250 births; 1959, about one maternal death in 2,000 live births. It has been calculated that, at the mid 1930s rate, some six million people now living in the Western world would be dead if it were not for the advances in medicine. Seventy per cent of the prescriptions written by doctors today could not have been written in 1935 and, evidence of the pace of progress, 45 per cent of today's prescriptions could not have been written even five years ago because the drugs did not exist.

* *People & Living*, United Nations, Sales No. 63.1.25.

Catastrophes have undoubtedly occurred; a United Nations publication* reports that deaths in the First World War amounted to 9,700,000 and in the Second World War to 54,800,000. Added together, however, these shocking figures are equivalent to only one year's increase in the world's population today. Any future nuclear war could, by comparison, reduce these figures to pin-pricks and the achievements of medicine over the last century could be wiped out.

A general comparison of the crude death rates for developed and underdeveloped countries masks the fact that deaths in the former are in the older age groups. The life expectancy of a youngster in Western Europe today is almost twice as long as that of his great-grand parents. The European population as a whole is growing older and although, compared with other less fortunate parts of the world, it is one of the healthiest continents, it maintains people with hereditary defects. Inherited disabilities can be passed on and in addition to the old-age spread more people's lives are being preserved by drugs. The pertinent question arises as to how far medical science can extend life expectancy. Occasional claims, such as the use of life-prolonging novopropain in Rumania, suggest a breakthrough. Dr. Willem Kolff, the American physician who invented the first effective artificial kidney, the dialysing machine, made it possible for people to live and work after receiving a kidney graft. Now we are on the verge of new hearts for old in plastic; silicone ball valves may replace Nature's pumping mechanism. Clinics merchandising human spare parts may be around the corner in A.D. 2000. The extent to which medical research can break through the 'old-age barrier' is difficult, if not impossible, to forecast. In Western countries where the average expectation of life still straddles the psalmist's three score years and ten, there appears to be little prospect of any significant extension of the old-age

* Source: *Economic Bulletin for Asia and the Far East.*

spread. A century hence, who knows?, a medical Shangri-La may be established. But the estimated increases of population for A.D. 2000 do not seriously consider any extension of life beyond today's average for industrialized countries.

Many technologically-based advances in medicine have been made available overnight, so to speak, to underdeveloped countries which have had static economies for centuries. People are living longer in unchanged, overcrowded conditions. But in these areas of massive population potential, life expectancy is still limited. Here the concern is with the 'middle-age spread'; it is unlikely that medicine can support an old-age spread before the year 2000. Consider these wretched life expectancies (average in years from birth): Borneo 29, Burma 34, Cambodia 40, India 42, Indonesia 39, Laos 34, Pakistan 35, Phillipines 44 and Thailand 40 compared with France 68 and the United Kingdom and U.S.A. at 71. Medical assistance, provided food is available, will enable such under-developed countries to gain on the pace-setters in the race to A.D. 2000, but the extension of life beyond an average of 70 is unlikely to be a major issue in this century for the increasing pressure of numbers may keep medicine fully occupied.

With an estimated 16 per cent of the world's population over the age of sixty-five in A.D. 2000, compared with some 3 per cent in 1900, life expectancies will increase slowly and disproportionately according to area. Whereas senescent Europe may be increasing the number of its geriatric units in the next few decades, the underdeveloped parts of the world may experience the pressure of youth. In some Latin American countried as much as 40 per cent of the population is under the age of fifteen today. Coale and Hoover* estimate that the proportion of children under fifteen in India in 1986, taking a low estimate only, will be a third (40 per cent might be a more

* Coale A. J. and Hoover E. M. *Population Growth & Economic Development in Low Income Countries.*

realistic figure) of the total population of the sub-continent. In South American countries with a small population base and attractive resources the problem may be overcome but in India and other overpopulated areas this unproductive, youthful pressure will be a decisive handicap to economic development. Every young mouth must be fed, although the hands will not be contributing to the expansion of the economy. A greater strain will be placed on the working population which could well do with procreating itself at a more leisurely pace.

These people produce the traditionally large family despite the decreasing demands of natural selection in lands which are being slowly saturated with a longer life expectancy. Some of these areas (Group 1) have an annual increase of between 3 and 4 per cent – a rate which can double the existing population within a generation. Here are the launching pads of humanity. Until these overpopulated countries can compensate for the increased expectation of life by reducing the birth rate, the fight to increase food production is to wage a losing battle. Only in the technologically developed areas of Europe, U.S.S.R., North and South America and Japan is the population increasing at a rate which can be handled, *at present*, without undue distress, if not with comfort. Crude birth rates per thousand of 19, 16 and 19 for France, United Kingdom and Japan respectively compare favourably with, for example, those of Borneo (46), Burma (44), Cambodia (47), Mainland China (37), Malaysia (44), Hong Kong (38), India (42), Indonesia (43), Laos (46), Pakistan (50), Phillipines (49), Thailand (47), and Mexico (46). The U.S.A., with a birth rate of 25 per thousand, shows the warning light, a possible future problem for many of the Group 3 countries. But the salvation of industrialized countries lies in their having paid the premium for education and industry; their dividends for long-term investment are in the form of fewer people enriched by relief from the burden of mere survival. For over-populated nations the increase in numbers can suck in the investment, human bankruptcy ensues and no dividends are payable.

CONCLUSION

It is generally accepted that a manageable increase in population in an expanding economy is desirable. Beyond a certain point, however, the increase becomes too heavy, the economy is sapped and the scourge of overpopulation takes over. The problem is to assess when that point, the optimum of population, has been reached for any given economy. Groups 2 and 3 are generally below or prodding the optimum point for their existing conditions. Groups 1 and 4 are beyond the optimum, some considerably in advance, others less so. Some argue that such population pressures can be relieved by the immediate introduction of industry and a swift expansion of education. This they maintain will bring about the demographic transition similar to that which occurred in England and Wales (Fig. 4). But the rate of population growth of the explosive countries today cannot be compared easily with the immediate past of England where a sharp increase in population went hand in hand with a rising tide of prosperity. This may not happen under present conditions in such countries as India and China because:

    (i) the increase was smaller and over a longer period of time,

    (ii) the economy was developed by trial and error at a slower rate; a twentieth-century way of life was not pasted on to an eighteenth- and nineteenth-century community,

    (iii) the increase occurred, after a short time-lag, with a *drop* in the birth rate,

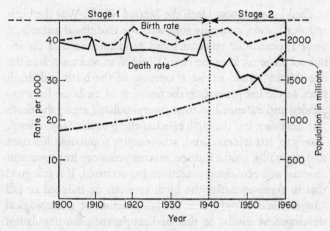

Fig. 5. Population Transition in Asia.

(iv) considerable emigration to the New World relieved
the pressure.

These factors checked the overpopulation of England and
Wales and similar countries.

There is no evidence to suggest that this demographic
transition is an automatic law to which today's overpopulated
nations must conform. They start with a much broader
population base than existed in Europe and consequently any
attempt at technological development would have to be on a
grandiose scale to precipitate the masses, in little over a generation, from a primitive agrarian economy to one in which
scientific farming and industry can run smoothly side by side.
Moreover, there is no indication, as yet, that birth rates are
likely to follow the downward trend of the population transition in Europe. Fig. 5 (compared with Fig. 4, page 15)
indicates that they are progressing through *Stage* 2. There is no
indication, as yet, that *Stages 3* and *4* (of Fig. 4) will be

reached by A.D. 2000. Until the Second World War the birth and death rates generally followed the traditional pattern of *Stage 1*, occasional epidemics and pandemics such as the influenza outbreak after the First World War, and malaria in the late thirties would devise a meeting of the birth and death rates. In the last generation the frontiers of medicine have expanded and extended to these overpopulated areas; the death rate has fallen but the birth rate has clung to the *Stage 1* level. The 'gap' has widened and, accordingly, population has risen sharply whilst, unlike Europe, no compensatory improvement in social and economic conditions has occurred. If it is argued that in these countries the birth rate can be induced to fall (*Stages 3* and *4*) only after the introduction of technological development similar to that of Europe, then the population increase between now and A.D. 2000 could effectively stifle any such attempts at progress.

Opinions are divided on such aspects of population theory. Time and differing circumstances add fresh fuel to the arguments. Aristotle and Plato dabbled in population predictions and through the centuries many theories have conformed to the demographic fashion of the time. To appreciate the present arguments related to the population explosion in the next few decades, a brief glimpse at various population theories, past and present, will be profitable.

Malthus was the first man to crystallize many of the previous arguments and present them forcefully for public consideration.

SOME QUESTIONS

1. How can a falling birth rate in a country result in an increased population?

2. What do you understand by 'technological birth control'?

3. Trace the development of 'death control' in Western countries in the last hundred years.

4. Why are underdeveloped, overpopulated countries unlikely to be concerned with the 'old-age spread' before A.D. 2000?

5. Explain why overpopulated countries may not follow a similar population transition to that which occurred in Europe.

DISCUSSION TOPICS

1. Why does an educated, technologically advanced country voluntarily restrict its population increase?

2. Discuss some of the sociological problems which already exist or may emerge in this country before A.D. 2000.

3: MALTHUS AND MARX

Thomas Robert Malthus (1766–1834), economist and clergyman, first expounded his ideas in his *Essay on Population* at the turn of the eighteenth century. His father and others (Condorcet and Godwin) in their search for a Utopian society were confounded by Malthus junior who was convinced that man would always be defiled by the curse of population increasing faster than food production. Originally he voiced the theory (modified later) that population could increase in a geometrical ratio (1, 2, 4, 8, 16, 32 ... while subsistence could progress only in an arithmetical ratio (1, 2, 3, 4, 5, 6 ...), subject to the qualification that new developments in agricultural techniques could, from time to time, broaden the base of the progression. The one would overhaul the other and, he believed, the positive checks of war, disease and famine would control population expansion to maintain the subsistence level. The resulting 'misery and vice', he gloomily forecast, would prevent the development of his father's dream of Utopia.

The abuse and criticism which greeted this pronouncement prompted him to revise his *Essay* and, after five years of painstaking research, he produced a modified theory which renewed the emphasis on population outstripping its means of subsistence. His mathematical progressions for population and resources were given less emphasis, although not abandoned, and more prominence was given to his recognition of 'moral restraint' in marriage as a preventive check to population increase. He was not an advocate of birth control in the modern sense of the term and would not have supported present practices. Thus the use of the term 'neo-Malthusian' for today's supporters of birth-control policies is a misnomer. However, Malthus was the supreme pessimist; he could not envisage man voluntarily controlling his increase and so the previous positive checks and their attendant 'misery and vice' were re-emphasized.

Of course, Malthus made the mistake of considering the consumers' rather than the producers' role. He could not foresee the tremendous effects of the Industrial Revolution, the opening up of extensive grainlands and other resources abroad together with the development of transport, and so, for Great Britain, his prophecy foundered although we still fight to bridge the trade 'gap'. 'Misery and vice' may still exist but in our society they do not have the same roots as Malthus predicted. He also opined, mistakenly, that the population expansion of his day was caused by increased births. In effect the birth rate was stable and the decrease in the death rate (*Stage 2*, Fig. 4) was the main cause. For many of the overpopulated lands of today, however, still in *Stage 2* of their development, his geometrical principle of progression could still be valid in broad outline. In fact Malthus envisaged the possibility that his 'principle' might not apply fully for some hundreds of years. A natural increase of 28 per thousand will double a given population group in 25 years. Ceylon with a birth rate of 42 and a death rate of 14 is an example of this rate of natural increase. Others are (birth and death rates respectively) Malaysia 44/12, Hong Kong 38/8, Phillipines 49/21, Singapore 48/9 and Mexico 46/13. These areas under their particular conditions at this particular time reflect the Malthusian principle of geometrical progression. Certain overpopulated areas may well be back to Malthus with a vengeance not only in terms of statistics but in relation to the inability to contain their natural increase. We have evidence that they are outstripping their means of subsistence and certainly the 'misery' and to some extent the 'vice' (although Malthus would not have supported the all-embracing, modern connotation of this term) are extant today. He was wrong also in his suggestion that better living conditions would stimulate births; we have seen that there is little evidence of significant increases in birth rates associated with improved living standards in any part of the world.

For his time, with the knowledge and statistics available, Malthus gave us some interesting population theories; extensive controversies still rage round him to this day. The passage of time has rejected much of his conjecture but the new population explosion is once more rousing the world and some of his basic pessimism, concerning the future of mankind, is once more evident. The prospect of a doubled population by A.D. 2000 has prompted some people masquerading as 'neo-Malthusians', to re-cast his principles in a modern mould.

NEO-MALTHUSIANISM?

Some neo-Malthusians maintain that foreign aid to underdeveloped countries aggravates rather than relieves their problem because, according to the Malthusian principle, population will increase to meet the improved subsistence level. Nothing, they might say, has been gained except an even bigger problem in the increased size of population. Such increases might lead to aggressive, expansionist policies and subsequent war. They often recall Hitler's cry for *Lebensraum* in a Germany which was hardly overpopulated by comparison with the Far East. Hitler's concern was really for power, not the peaceful alleviation of population pressure. This theory is based on the assumption, not universally accepted, that population will chase the subsistence level.

A similar argument is levelled against the giving of medical aid because the necessary social and economic progress does not keep pace with increased population and so the population pyramid has insecure foundations; the structure becomes top-heavy. A very effective answer is that, for some countries, reducing the mortality rate especially of young people on the verge of lending a hand, for the first time, in the economy is the primary step towards expanding its labour force. Pre-war India spent nearly a quarter of its income in rearing children who never survived adolescence and were lost at a time when they should have been a valuable capital asset. Moreover, no nation can build a sound economy on unhealthy bodies.

Other arguments point to the example of Europe. If in various ways the overpopulated nations can be given a higher standard of living, *Stages 3* and *4* will be reached. Relieve the pangs of hunger and birth pangs will be fewer. It was suggested in the last chapter that the conditions to fulfil this theory are hardly likely to be satisfied by the year 2000. Moreover, even in industrialized countries, the birth rate, although relatively stable, is still rising. The birth rates in industrialized countries began to decline a century ago. On this basis China, now at 700 millions, could well reach 4000 millions before the decline in birth rates could effect the necessary control and by that time the damage would be done. In arguments of this type there are often too many parallels drawn with the West. The twain may well meet in some respects but the development of a Cambodian need not necessarily be in the same direction as that of the cockney.

Some mis-named neo-Malthusians advocate birth control in an attempt to slow down the rate of increase. Their aim is not to reduce populations to a stagnant state but to plan for a manageable increase. In opposition there are those who will not, or cannot, sanction birth control in population theories. Apart from religious taboos it is often claimed, and there is truth in this, that uneducated masses cannot easily appreciate and practice this form of limitation even though it is evident how closely the progress they need is tied to a drop in birth rates.

Then there is the modern pessimist who fears that an unproductive ageing population will be a burden on the economy. But if the economy can be allowed to expand by a reduction in birth rates this weight can be more easily carried. Undoubtedly the younger people will shoulder a heavier responsibility but, in the process, they will have been relieved of the struggle for maturity and may be better equipped to support their elders.

Another favourite suggestion is to drag the people off the land as the panacea to overpopulation. But urbanization is no answer without industrialization which, in turn, is dependent on the inevitably slow development of education together with the liberal provision of capital and resources. Urbanization alone merely adds weight to the social problems of overpopulation. Extreme neo-Malthusians see a great danger here. They visualize pressure points expanding and engulfing the industrialized nations; they fear a depression in the general standard of living, contemplate a fraying of the fabric of law and order, and look nuclear warfare in the face, these gloomy prophets of doom.

Carr-Saunders has rationalized much of this neo-Malthusian controversy in supporting the theory that man tends to restrict his numbers to the economics of a given situation. He accepts Malthus's contention that man increases his numbers at a quicker rate than his means of subsistence but rejects 'misery and vice' as the check for population expansion. In considering the optimum population for a given economy he prefers to rely on man's natural adaptability to accommodate the fluctuations within any social order.

MARX

Communist writers often argue that overpopulation and associated misery are the result of the maldistribution of resources within society. Reorganize the social structure, ease the pressure of overpopulated areas (political expansion with no peaceful co-existence?), they say, and production will out-strip the capacity to multiply. Marx and Malthus would never have seen eye to eye. Malthus was obsessed with the problem of overpopulation – Marx declined to recognize it. But in attempting to disprove the validity of capitalism, Marx ignored the fact that overpopulation in socialist states can stem from exactly the same causes as those under capitalism. China proves the point. So concerned was he with proving capitalism to be the parent of overpopulation that he ignored the demo-graphic factors responsible for population growth.

According to Marx, the labour of man is the basis of wealth and so the greater the population, if organized on socialist lines, the greater the well-being of man; on this basis the term 'overpopulation' is foreign to his vocabulary. Such a lack of recognition of the causes of overpopulation is dangerous. It can lead to a niggardly and precarious existence for the masses at a minimum subsistence level. Of course, Marx would not have subscribed to this view for he maintained that efficient socialist management should be able to cope adequately with population increases and, moreover, provide a better standard of living. On this basis the Chinese government abandoned, in the late fifties, their official support for a birth-control policy except where family planning was considered to be necessary for the health of mother and child. They decided that overpopulation was not a bogey and could be absorbed adequately by the industrial 'Great Leap Forward'. Certainly Mainland China has fared better under the communists than under the previous régime but a proper realization of the causes and effects of overpopulation is required. There have been recent suggestions that the Chinese government is once again examining the need for an officially supported birth-control policy. Such modern thinking, with less attention to political dogma, would produce even better results. For a country like U.S.S.R., of course, the Marxist population theory is still valid. Her vast resources need more man and womanpower if the development of her empty spaces is to be achieved, provided the Chinese do not spill over into the tempting emptiness of Siberian Russia. Apart from any difference in their interpetations of communism these two massive nations have sufficient differences in their population structure and birth rates to keep them apart. An expanding population is only the concomitant of wealth under certain economic conditions – those of Russia, not of China.

CONCLUSION

Malthus's assertion that man's capacity to multiply is much greater than his capacity to increase his means of subsistence, by the controversy it provoked, was responsible for stimulating much of the subsequent research into population problems. But the failure of two of the main criteria in his thesis, those of continence and war, to keep population in check would have made him even gloomier. He never envisaged nuclear war, of course, or the extent of the predicted population expansion for the next generation. It is to be hoped that no future nuclear war will prevent the overpopulated lands continuing to outstrip their means of subsistence. Although vindicated in modern eyes he would have been the last person to have rejoiced in the mushroom cloud acting as a positive check to the mushroom crowd.

SOME QUESTIONS

1. Comment on the fallacies of Malthus's population theories.

2. Who are the *neo-Malthusians* and why are they so called?

3. Explain and comment on the Marxist attitude to overpopulation.

DISCUSSION TOPICS

1. 'Malthus, Marx and others have differed in their attitudes to the increase in the world's population but, at least, they showed concern for the problem. But to many others the problem is not their concern; it lies elsewhere. Here are the mass of the men-in-the-street, the live and let die brigade.'

Discuss ways in which the population problem can be brought home to Tom, Dick and Harry.

2. 'All men are equal, but some are more equal than others.'

4: THE PROBLEM AREAS

The proportion of Europeans as a percentage of world population is receding very quickly. The underdeveloped countries grow at a faster rate, approximately 3 per cent per annum, compared with the slower increase, about 1 per cent per annum, in Western Europe. Figs. 6, 7 and 8 represent the

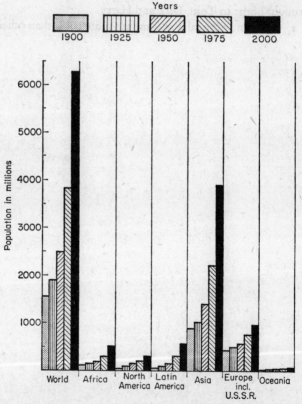

Fig. 6. Population of the Continents of the World A.D. 1900–2000.

Fig. 7. Estimated Percentage Population Increases in each Continent. *

Years	World	Africa	North America	Latin America	Asia	Europe incl. U.S.S.R.	Oceania
1900–25	23	22	56	57	19	19	57
1925–50	31	35	33	65	35	14	36
1950–75	53	52	43	86	60	31	59
1975–2000	64	71	30	95	75	26	40

Fig. 8. Percentage of World Population Contained in each Continent
with Projections for 1975 and 2000. *

1900	100·0	7·7	5·2	4·1	55·3	27·3	0·4
1925	100·0	7·7	6·6	5·2	53·5	26·5	0·5
1950	100·0	8·0	6·7	6·5	55·2	23·0	0·5
1975	100·0	7·9	6·3	7·9	57·7	19·6	0·5
2000	100·0	8·2	5·0	9·4	61·8	15·1	0·5

varied and disproportionate increase in the peoples of the world in the present century.

The bar graph and supporting figures indicate how the increase of the world's population has divided its inhabitants into two unequal sections:

(i) *Groups 1* and *4* (pages 10 & 11) represent the demographically unstable, underdeveloped countries comprising over two-thirds of the total world population including Asia (with the exceptions of U.S.S.R. and Japan), the greater part of Africa and tropical Latin America.

(ii) *Groups 2* and *3* (pages 10 & 11) are the demographically stable, technologically developed nations of Europe, North America, U.S.S.R., the temperate zones of Latin America, Japan and Oceania (which includes Australia and New Zealand).

The difference between these two main groupings will

* Medium Assumptions. *Source: U.N.O. Population Studies No. 28*

become even more pronounced by the year 2000. Europe's contribution to the world's population will have dropped from 27·3 per cent to 15·1 per cent in this century. Asia's percentage will increase from about 55 per cent to 62 per cent, any illusions concerning the seemingly small increase in this contribution being swept away by a glance at Fig. 6. The almost doubled population of Latin America in this century will be held in relative comfort on a small population base whilst Africa's share may hover around 8 per cent. North America reverts, in A.D. 2000, to its share in 1900, its population percentage increase showing an overall decline over the century.

Asia, excluding U.S.S.R. and Japan, which now has some 1,700 millions, may have reached 2,210 millions by 1975 and nearly 4,000 millions in A.D. 2000. These figures, based on United Nations projections, assume that after 1975 birth rates may show a tendency to fall and that death rates will continue their present downward trend.

The net result of this complex pattern of differential growth has been to increase the share of the world's population in the underdeveloped countries at the expense of that of the technologically advanced countries with a greater distinction probably becoming more evident the nearer A.D. 2000 is reached. Moreover, the state of imbalance is likely to get even worse beyond the turn of the century. N. Keyfitz predicts* that just after A.D. 2040 there will be, with present and projected trends, 12,000 millions . . . 'We need not go on to the fifteen or so doublings that would end with each person having one square foot of the earth's land surface nor to the fifteen or so beyond that which would bring the weight of human beings to that of the earth itself. . . . .' By A.D. 2041, Keyfitz envisages the following surges in population in the underdeveloped areas:

* *United Nations Conference on the Application of Science & Technology for the Benefit of the Less Developed Areas.* 1963. Paper B/10.

Fig. 9. Estimated World Populations by Continents A.D. 1961 and A.D. 2041. *

Year	1961		2041	
Area	Millions	Per Cent	Millions	Per Cent
Largely Europe	500	17	1,110	10
Largely U.S.A. and U.S.S.R.	500	17	1,800	15
Largely Asia	2,000	66	9,000	75
Totals	3,000	100	11,910	100

With this possible pattern of the future development of mankind the pressure points and other rapidly expanding areas require investigation.

CHINA'S CHOICE: A CHALLENGE?

With about 700 millions China holds a little less than half of the 1,700 millions of people in Asia. The Chinese population is expanding rapidly, a trend which appears to be inevitable unless a major catastrophe introduces a Malthusian check to raise the death rates for there seems to be no official support for birth control policies. In considering such future population trends demographers are hampered by the doubtful validity of population returns in China (see Appendix I). Nevertheless, in view of the explosive nature of the problem an attempt at population prediction must be made. The Communist régime has developed industrialization with particular and successful emphasis on heavy industry, despite the relative paucity of mineral resources, and population predictions must consider any resultant effects. If the demographic transition of established industrialized nations is followed, then a lowered birth rate will have to be taken into account. This possibility,

* United Nations Conference on the Application of Science & Technology for the Benefit of the Less Developed Areas. 1963. Paper B/10.

however, could be offset by a further reduction in the death rate giving, perhaps by the end of the century, a rate of natural increase of a little under 2 per cent. Such a projection, presuming that the Chinese maintain their vague attitude to birth control, would give a total population of some 1,850 millions in A.D. 2000 which would represent 30 per cent of the world's population compared with the present 22 per cent. By the end of the century the Chinese could equal the total population of Asia today and result in every other Asian and every third person in the world being of Chinese origin.

China's problem, certainly to outsiders, is that her population base is too large to start with. If social and economic conditions were ideal her 700 millions could be coped with adequately for the average population density of 568 persons per square kilometre of *arable* land is not excessive compared, say, with the density of 1,783 in Japan. But crude birth and death rates of 37 and 17 respectively give a 2·4 per cent rate of natural increase which is too high for the existing population base. At present this gives a net annual rate of increase of 20 per 1,000 resulting in an annual growth at present of about 12 millions, over half of which is carried by the already overpopulated rural areas. There is a tendency, common to many parts of the world, for a drift of people from rural to urban areas to the extent of some 5 millions each year. Some large cities are developing; in the western provinces Kalgan mushroomed from a quarter of a million in 1949 to top the million mark in 1957. Canton and Shanghai have become 'shapeless, soulless cities, peopled with blue ants, criss-crossed by human-drawn vehicles'.* Even so the balance is adversely redressed by the rate of natural increase and so urban populations represent only about 15 per cent of the total Chinese population.

After forty years of war the Chinese Communist collectivization programme has made considerable advances in

* A. Fabre-Luce in *Men or Insects?*

agricultural production. Much of the dead weight of idle and partially employed labour, the soul-destroying plight of half of the Asian peasantry, has been utilized in reclaiming and fertilizing marginal land. Irrigation, afforestation and anti-erosion measures, aided by the introduction of modern tools and appliances, have brought about an agricultural revolution by which the productivity of farm labour has risen to such an extent that the Chinese government seems to have rejected fears of overpopulation. With Marxist optimism they seem convinced that agricultural production will exceed the future demands of population growth. In fact various attempts to promote birth control policies have been abandoned or slowed down. Whether this is to attune the rejection of peaceful co-existence in political practice with the Marxist theory of over-population which advocates the redistribution of people within *or* outside her boundaries is, perhaps, the burning question of our day.

THE PREGNANT SMOCK OF INDIA

'India today presents a very mixed picture of hope and anguish, of remarkable advances and at the same time of inertia, of a new spirit and also the dead hand of the past and of privilege, of an overall and growing unity and many disruptive influences.'   *Jawaharlal Nehru. 1959*

Thus Nehru, one of India's greatest sons, saw his country as a mosaic of massive complexities. This country breeds impressive statistics, often difficult to appreciate. It is a land of villages, three-quarters of a million of them, with here and there teeming towns and cities. Calcutta is aptly designated 'the capital of overpopulation'. With 450 million people, in-creasing at 2 per cent per annum, India is the world's largest democracy, two-thirds the size of Europe but with an annual income no greater than £25 per head. Here, then, is an agrarian country making tremendous efforts, although constantly thwarted with setbacks, for an economic breakthrough. Her recurring problem is that each economic success is nullified by increased population pressure. The average density of 245 persons per square kilometre of *arable* land is not excessive but this masks the chronic congestion of pressure points such as those in the Ganges basin and delta. Crude birth and death rates of 42 and 29 respectively give a natural rate of increase of about 2 per cent and, as in China, this is too high for a large and existing population base. India is following the typical *Stage 2* (Fig. 5, page 23) development with birth rates failing to follow the downward trend of death rates which fell from 44·4 per thousand in 1890 to 31·2 in 1930 whilst the birth rate never moved below 45 per 1,000 over this period. In the last four decades the birth and death rates have dropped by only 3 and 2 per 1,000 respectively and so the 'gap' has failed to close and population surges ahead.

It has been estimated that if fertility remains at the present level and the death rate falls by at least forty per cent – a reasonable possibility – by 1986 India's population will be 775 millions, nearly doubled in less than a generation. That death rates can be severely curtailed in a short period of time, thus adding to the population burden, is evidenced by the example of Ceylon. D.D.T., introduced to the Far East extensively in 1940, effected control of malaria and brought the Singhalese death rate down from 20·6 per 1,000 in 1940 to 13·2 in 1948. When India gained independence in 1947 the population was estimated at 345 millions. Within ten years it had stretched to 400 millions. Two significant factors in this increase were the reduced rate of infant mortality following the spread of post-war medical benefits and, for the first time, average life expectancy spilled over into middle age at forty-two years whilst birth rates remained stable. The scene was set for the vicious onslaught of numbers. Some 5 millions per year were added between 1950–55. The annual increase rose to about 7 millions from 1955 to 1960 and, by the mid sixties, some 10 millions annually, so that by 1970, with no significant decline in the birth rates, about 550 millions will be scratching at or below subsistence level. This represents nearly a 60 per cent increase in population in twenty-three years, equivalent to the present population of Latin America.

India has faced this threat by organizing three Five-Year Plans in the post-war period to increase food production in an attempt to cater for population increases and, additionally, to improve the subsistence level. At best, however, the subsistence level is being maintained only. By 1961, the termination of the second Five-Year Plan, only about three-fifths of the agricultural targets were achieved and the third Plan, finishing in 1966, has watched its production targets gradually slipping beyond reach in a country where over 80 per cent of the population, mostly illiterate, live on and feed off the land. Even if any subsequent Plans were to achieve success, the sub-continent is faced with this continued pressure of population, providing the reduced mortality rate is not reversed by starvation and malnutrition. Under these overcrowded conditions only about 10 per cent of India's national income would be available for investment in production because the increased population would suck in money for essential but non-productive investments in the social services. The pressure can be relieved only by increasing the existing efforts to extend birth control. To quote Nehru again, 'Population control will not solve all our problems, but other problems will not be solved without it.' Artificial restriction is, perhaps, the price the Indians have to pay for Western interference in removing some of Nature's positive checks.

THE JAPANESE STRAIT-JACKET

Since 1950 Japan, an increasingly urbanized nation, has restricted its population by means of a falling birth rate, as a result of a higher literacy level, the dogged pursuit of industrialization, and birth control. But, with an average of 1,783 persons per square kilometre of *arable* land, it is a nation in a straight-jacket.

The crude birth and death rates of 19 and 8 respectively reflect the typical western pattern of a 1·1 per cent rate of natural increase. Japan is the only overpopulated Asiatic country which has copied the demographic transition of Europe and succeeded in closing the flood-gates of population increase, for the time being at any rate, within a very short space of time – by intensive attention to birth control. It is a country which gets things done quickly. Her industrial revolution did not begin until about 1890, some 130 years after Great Britain. Prior to this her population had been static at about 30 millions for a considerable period of time. By 1920, 55 millions had been reached and the end of the Second World War saw 72 millions. The boom in post-war births, typical of the West, lasted until about 1950 when births were up to 34 per 1,000 and the 84 millions mark was reached. And then the Japanese, with characteristic efficiency, decided to loosen the strait-jacket by reducing the number of births. Abortion and sterilization had been legalized in 1948 and birth control was preached as government policy. The effects were soon to be seen.

Within ten years the birth rate was nearly halved to 19 per 1,000 and the rate of natural increase had dropped to 11 per 1,000 – a low figure even by Western standards – so that the period to 1960 saw a retarded increase to 93·5 millions. With the relative affluence of the sixties, however, there has been a tendency for the birth rate to rise, but now that the population cycle is complete there is little likelihood that it will return to the basic Asian pattern. Japanese families have tasted the benefits of planned parenthood. Moreover, they recognize that overpopulation hangs like a sinister shadow over the economy and still poses problems, for Japan faces the possibility of 110 millions in 1970 and 153 millions by A.D. 2000. The reduced birth rate also means fewer productive workers in the immediate future to support an increasing segment of older people whose life expectancy of sixty-six is little below that of Western Europe.

Another important problem is the increasing congestion in urban areas. About three-quarters of recent increases have been in the main urban centres such as Tokyo, a city of 10 million people living shoulder to shoulder under the shadow of seismic disturbance, and Osaka. But rural life is still as cramped as ever.

LATIN AMERICAN RUMBLINGS

Latin America, comprising Mexico, Central and South America, presents a different problem to that of India or China. Population densities are much lower and certainly resources are much greater. For centuries this undiscovered corner of the world remained sparsely peopled. It was not until the middle of the nineteenth century that immigration made any significant contribution to the increased population of the various South American states. Indeed, the powder of the explosive period is still in the air for the decade 1950–60 saw about 75 million births and some 31 million deaths, giving an excess of births over deaths of 44 millions and representing a 94 per cent increase for the period. Thus the 162 millions in Latin America in 1950 rose to 206 millions in 1960. United Nations estimates suggest that 1970 will see 265 millions which will expand to 592 millions in A.D. 2000. This expansion is likely to occur in the demographically unstable tropical states for the temperate zone countries are conforming to the pattern of Western stability in population growth.

This century may well see a doubling of Latin America's percentage of world population from 4·1 per cent in 1900 to 9·4 per cent in A.D. 2000 and the cause is the familiar 'gap' between birth and death rates. In tropical areas birth rates oscillate between 40 and 49 per 1,000 whilst death rates are falling. Only Argentina and Uruguay display the Western trend; elsewhere the fertility rate is twice as high as that of Europe. And so the economies of the various countries have to support an expanding stratum of unproductive children. The potential carrying capacity of the land is high but, for the most part, unrealized. It is reported* that north-eastern Brazil experiences famine despite its ability to cater adequately for many more than its 66 million inhabitants. But with 42 per cent of its population under fifteen years of age and only a half of its adults being literate, it is obvious why resources are not adequately utilized.

Another problem is the tendency of people to concentrate in a few large urban areas, often capital cities. A quarter of Latin Americans live in urban concentrations of at least 20,000 and a fifth in cities no less than 200,000 in size. Significantly in the last decade, the increase in rural populations has been only 1 per cent compared with 5 per cent in urban areas and it is estimated that urban populations will treble in the next twenty-five years whilst rural populations will increase by less than 30 per cent. The land, the panacea for overpopulation, is being shunned.

There are considerable differences in the population densities of the variegated pattern of Latin America states ranging from the Puerto Rican (Latin American by temperament if not strictly by position) density of 600 per square mile to 4 per

* *Basic Study No. 7.* United Nations.

square mile in Bolivia. To add to the complexity the higher densities are not always in the best endowed areas and the fastest rates of increase have been spawned, sometimes, from countries with a small population base. Colombia, for example, has the highest growth rate of population in Latin America at over 3 per cent.

But with 15 per cent of the earth's surface housing only 7 per cent of its inhabitants, the picture is far from depressing. The rich, oil-lubricated economy of Venezuela, for example, supports only fifteen people per square mile, admittedly unevenly distributed. Indeed the echoes of the recent cries of overpopulation are still reverberating from the Andes and must sound strange as they ripple out to the Far East. The Indians and Chinese may well regard the heavier concentrations as comparative smudges easily erased by the handy resources. Certainly the arid zones of Colombia, Peru, Paraguay and Chile need attention if and when the future populations demand it. Similarly the Amazonian jungles will require considerable capital for the utilization of apparently luxurious, but often sterile, soils.

Latin America needs controlled population growth before the roots of overpopulation become too deep-seated otherwise nearly 600 millions by A.D. 2000 could follow the pattern of the Far East. With regulated growth this number can be handled for, adequately developed, the land and resources are available.

SOME QUESTIONS

1. Analyze the reasons why the peoples of the world are split into two major groups, the demographically stable and unstable.

2. Compare the Indian and Chinese governments' attitudes to the problem of overpopulation.

3. Comment on the ways in which the Japanese have brought their population growth under control since the war.

DISCUSSION TOPICS

1. 12,000 millions in A.D. 2041! A baby born today could witness this growth. Imagine the possible political repercussions if this prediction were to materialize.

2. 'Canton and Shanghai have become shapeless, soulless cities, peopled with blue ants, criss-crossed by human-drawn vehicles.'

Discuss the social problems associated with such urban pressure points.

5: HUNGER KILLS: MALNUTRITION KILLS MORE

'The litany of hunger is expressed in a saying in the East:

> 'Better to walk than to run:
> Better to sit than to walk:
> Better to sleep than to sit:
> Better to die than to wake:

'It does not shout from the headlines like famine, nor scandalize us like the walking skeletons of Belsen. It is the creeping death of progressive malnutrition, of people dragging out the years of a stunted life, without the energy or will to help themselves.'*

This tragedy is accentuated by the gap between the 'have' and 'have not' nations. Ten per cent of the human race live off 60 per cent of the world's income whilst 60 per cent of the people subsist on only 10 per cent of the world's income. Most of these unfortunates are in the Far East and they compare very unfavourably with those in North America (7 per cent of the world's population) who enjoy 40 per cent of the world's income. If population outstrips subsistence this gap may widen even further at a time when newly emerging states are casting hungry eyes on their more fortunate neighbours. Hunger can be the springboard of war which may be averted only by a more even distribution of the world's income.

The vocabulary of hunger requires definition. A *calorie* measures the energy-producing value of food and *hunger*, or *undernutrition*, refers to the inadequacy of calorie intake of the body compared with *malnutrition* which results from poor

* Professor Ritchie Calder.

quality or unbalanced diets. Hunger reduces body weight, hampers physical activity, encourages lassitude and, in children, retards physical growth. Malnutrition can spark off similar symptoms. It is often difficult to differentiate between hunger and malnutrition; indeed they can be complementary for the hungry person may lack a balanced diet and an over-stuffed child, lacking a balanced diet, may suffer from malnutrition.

The mathematics of hunger make dismal reading. B. R. Sen, Director-General of the Food and Agriculture Organization, estimates* that 60 per cent of the people in the under-developed parts of the world, housing two-thirds of the world's population, suffer from hunger, malnutrition or both. Add to this the ill-fed peoples in other parts of the world and about a half of the human race are found to be hungry or mal-nourished. The hungry ones, those who do not get enough to eat as distinct from those who get sufficient quantity but lacking in quality, represent between 10 and 15 per cent of the world's population. It is reasonable to assume, therefore, that between 400 and 500 million people, equivalent to two-thirds the population of Europe, go hungry.

WHAT DO PEOPLE NEED TO EAT?

Fig. 10 emphasizes the extent of calorie deficiency in the world and should be read in conjunction with Fig. 3 (page 8) to correct irregularities in the main regional classifications.

These comparisons indicate that the technologically ad-vanced nations of Europe, North America and Oceania aver-age about a twenty per cent excess of calorie requirements, Latin America and Africa generally satisfy the required level but the Far East calorie requirement is deficient by about 11 per cent, sometimes stretched over the whole year or

* *Third World Food Survey*, F.A.O., 1963.

Fig. 10. Comparison of the Daily Intake of Calories by Regions.*

Region	Calorie Supplies	Calorie Requirements
Far East	2,070	2,300
Africa	2,360	2,400
Latin America	2,470	2,400
Europe	3,040	2,600
North America	3,120	2,600
Oceania	3,250	2,600

* *Third World Food Survey*, F.A.O., 1963.

Note : The calorie requirement represents the average need in calories of a healthy person – based on the F.A.O. international requirement scale. In using these comparisons, allowance must be made for differing needs, e.g. a teenage athlete or a nursing mother in Europe may require at least 4,000 calories per day whilst an elderly, sedentary worker might well exist on a little over half of this intake. Moreover, climate and geographical location play a significant part in determining calorie requirements.

emphasized in the pre-harvest void. Even in Latin America and Africa, with an apparently satisfactory level, there are areas of malnutrition and hunger resulting from the maldistribution of supplies or climatic irregularities in areas where stocks of food are insufficient, or non-existent, to bridge a lean year.

The calorie requirement level should be compared with Fig. 11 detailing the regional shares of the world's agricultural production. It is evident that the Far East, the area with the greatest deficiency, has, relative to population, a meagre proportion of the world's agricultural production.

A balanced diet requires various kinds of food in which two main energy suppliers are important. The *carbohydrates* – starch and sugars, etc. – are found in bread, milk, cereals, peas, beans, cakes, jam . . . and *fatty foods* include butter, cheese, bacon, and peanuts. The body builders are the *proteins* found in meat, fish and eggs. To complete the balance certain vitamins, mineral

Fig. 11. Regional Percentage Shares of the World's Agricultural Production and Population.*

Region	Agricultural Production %	Population %
Western Europe	15	11
E. Europe (incl. U.S.S.R.)	17	10
North America	21	7
Latin America	8	7
Far East	28	53
Near East	4	4
Africa	4	7
Oceania	3	1

* United Nations, Basic Study No. 7.

salts and water are necessary. Most balanced diets ensure that the carbohydrates play a major role, provided the fat and protein levels are adequate. Fig. 12, however, illustrates the unbalanced nature of diets in various regions of the world.

Thus the North American eats about six times as much top-quality food as the peasant of the Far East. Represented diagrammatically the difference is shown in Fig. 13, page 52.

Most countries rely on the basic cereals and starchy foods, supplemented and increasingly replaced in richer nations by a greater proportion of proteins and other protective foods. Figs. 12 and 13 illustrate that diets in the Far East are badly balanced and, for the most part, minimal only. Diets in the Near East and Africa show a little less dependence on carbohydrates but the proportion is still too high. The alarming trend is that, whereas other regions are improving or maintaining a satisfactory calorie and protein intake, the Far East has regressed in the post-war period owing, no doubt, to the increased pressure of population. Fig. 14 illustrates this problem.

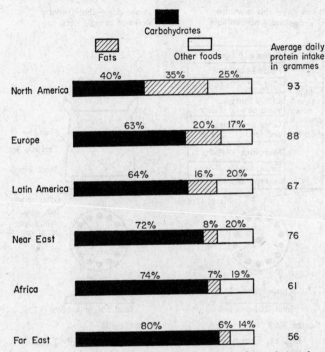

Fig. 12. Average Daily Calorie Intake Per Head of Population from Carbohydrates, Fats and Other Foods.

Except in the Far East the calorie intakes are reasonably adequate in the worst cases but the deficiency in proteins, especially of animal origin, is much more serious and in Africa, Latin America and the Far East the protein intake is much lower than that for developed regions. Animal protein level in North America is 66 grammes per day compared with 8 grammes in the Far East.

It is a sad comment on our times that the new American 'non-food' (a concoction of cellulose) should have been hailed as a 'miraculous scientific discovery'. It has plenty of bulk and

In one day— this is what a city-dwelling American eats

In one day— this is what a workman in India eats

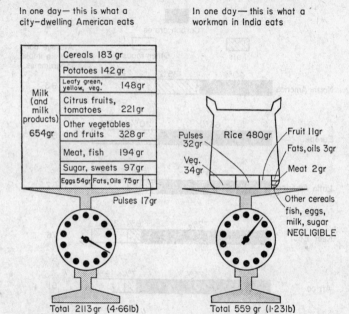

Milk (and milk products) 654gr	Cereals 183 gr
	Potatoes 142 gr
	Leafy green, yellow, veg. 148gr
	Citrus fruits, tomatoes 221gr
	Other vegetables and fruits 328gr
	Meat, fish 194 gr
	Sugar, sweets 97 gr
	Eggs 54gr Fats, Oils 75gr

Pulses 17gr

Pulses 32gr | Rice 480gr | Fruit 11gr
Veg. 34gr

Fats, oils 3gr

Meat 2gr

Other cereals fish, eggs, milk, sugar NEGLIGIBLE

Total 2113gr (4·66lb)

Total 559 gr (1·23lb)

Source: *FAO*

Source: *USDA*

Fig. 13. Comparison of American and Indian Daily Diets.

Fig. 14. Daily Calorie and Protein Intake By Regions.★

Region	Calories		Total Proteins (grammes)	
	Pre-war	Recent	Pre-war	Recent
Far East	2,120	2,070	63	56
Africa	2,180	2,360	61	61
Latin America	2,140	2,470	66	67
Europe	2,850	3,040	85	88
North America	3,140	3,120	89	93

★ *Source:* Sukhatme, P. W. *The World's Hunger and Future Needs in Food Supplies: Journal of the Royal Statistical Society.* Series A. (General.) Vol. 124.

no nutritional value whatsoever but prevents the stomach from feeling neglected. This is the scientists' answer to the diseases of the rich: an attempt to *reduce* animal protein intake and still allow the psychological satisfaction of mechanical eating.

The statistics for China are, as usual, dubious but it is possible that the average calorie intake is about 2,100 compared with 1,950 for India and Pakistan; but the Chinese probably absorb this extra energy by their greater labour encouraged by a more temperate climate.

The daily protein, especially animal, intake is the best way of measuring the nutritional quality of diet. The developed countries have a daily *animal* protein intake of at least 50 grammes compared with the 8 grammes of the Far East. Between these extremes the intake varies. In tropical Latin America it is from 15 to 30 grammes daily. Vegetable protein helps to compensate but is no adequate substitute for that of animal origin. In the United Kingdom, for example, 59 per cent of the average daily 85 grammes is animal protein compared with only 10 per cent of the daily 50 grammes in India. Indeed about 70 per cent of the world's supply of protein comes from vegetable sources; the rest is of animal origin. This ratio needs to be reversed in favour of the underdeveloped countries where grains, the staple food, are the major source of protein. Pulses, oil seeds, nuts and starchy roots also contribute to a lesser extent. The main food surpluses in the world are mainly cereals – wheat and coarse grains – but the primary need is for protein-rich foods which do not figure so prominently in these surpluses. Fig. 15 illustrates this dilemma.

DIET AND DEFICIENCY

This variety of statistical evidence bears witness to the inadequacy in quality and quantity of the diets of people in

Fig. 15. Daily Protein Intake Per Head of Regional Populations.*

Area	Total Protein	Animal Protein	Animal as a proportion of total (%)
	Grammes per head per day		
W. Europe	83	39	47
E. Europe & U.S.S.R.	94	33	35
N. America	93	66	71
Oceania	94	62	66
Latin America	67	24	36
Far East	56	8	14
Near East	76	14	18
Africa	61	11	18

* Source : F.A.O. State of Food & Agric. 1964.

underdeveloped areas. Hunger often screams its headlines to the world as relief organizations rush supplies to famine-stricken points. But malnutrition creeps quietly and insidiously indoors. Health and vitality are impaired and a number of *deficiency diseases* are closely associated.

The causes of malnutrition are difficult to trace. Whereas hunger is easily identified with an aching stomach, malnutrition has many contributory factors. We have seen that proteins, especially animal, are important to the body but so are minerals and vitamins. The proportion of calories from cereals, sugar and starchy roots also plays a major role. The problem of malnutrition is to recognize any state of imbalance in diet and to prescribe accordingly – more and, usually, better food.

Most of the deficiency diseases are found in the under-developed countries because they are associated with the lack of proteins and vitamins. In S.E. Asia alone there are 1,000 millions of people who have less than ten grammes of animal protein per day and when other areas are taken into account, about half the people in the world suffer at some stage in their lives from malnutrition. Dr Sen maintains that there is probably no African child who has not suffered from a deficiency disease at least once in his childhood and there is accumulating evidence that deficiency diseases are prevalent also in many parts of Latin America in addition to the Far East – in fact, all those areas where food supplies are deficient in animal protein.

DEFICIENCY AND DISEASE

Ignorance and superstition play a significant rôle in deficiency diseases. Often the sufferers do not realize the importance of a balanced diet and traditional attitudes are difficult to uproot. Disease-ridden cows are revered and starved in India; Muslims will not eat pork. Evil spirits in pure well water drive villagers to the good spirits in polluted ditch-water. Smallpox vaccinations in India are often accepted only if the medical people call them 'Kali vaccinations' because that powerful goddess is believed to be in charge of smallpox. In certain parts of Africa eggs are not eaten by women for fear of infertility. Traditional methods of cooking often waste valuable nutrients and are unhygienic, but villagers are loathe to adopt new and better techniques. The answer lies in the slow progress of education for living.

Deficiency diseases spring from two main dietary gaps – protein/calorie malnutrition and vitamin/mineral deficiencies.

Kwashiorkor (known to Africans as 'the sickness by which the first baby dies when the next baby is born') is the disease of young toddlers in S.E. Asia and many parts of Africa. It develops from the swift change from weaning to a starchy, vegetable diet. Swollen limbs, wasted muscles, skin sores and rashes rack the child. The symptoms and causes of *nutritional marasmus* are similar and *anaemia* and *hookworm* are secondary diseases commonly associated with both of these.

Vitamin deficiency diseases, of course, are often found side by side with protein deficiency diseases. A sixth of the world's population suffers from *trachoma*, an eye disease often causing blindness, to which a deficiency of Vitamin A_1 can be a contributory factor. *Beri-beri*, caused by thiamine deficiency, is the lot of those who subsist mainly on white or polished rice. Paralysis and general stupor result. Maize eaters are liable to *pellagra* which scales their skin, encourages diarrhoea, leads to severe depression and, often, insanity. *Goitres* signify a deficiency of iodine or iron in diets.

In addition to these specific deficiency diseases, malnutrition lowers the resistance of the host to many other diseases and infections. To this sorrowful list add *yaws* which cover the patient with boils, the crippling *bilharziasis*, *tuberculosis* and the 10 millions suffering from *leprosy*. And then consider the debilitating effect of *malaria* to which a fifth of the world's people are exposed, include the tsetse-fly disease of *trypanosomiasis* (sleeping sickness) to which East and West Africans are especially susceptible, and the list is yet incomplete.

Over a half of the world's people suffer at some time in their lives from one or other, or many, of these diseases and this is bad enough. But the social effects of persistent malnutrition are incalculable. There is a lack of energy and initiative, a refusal to face physical or intellectual effort. This is at a time when the underdeveloped lands need all these qualities for the successful delivery of their increasing numbers from the body- and soul-destroying effects of hunger and malnutrition.

SOME QUESTIONS

1. What is the difference between hunger and malnutrition?

2. Explain the predicament of the peoples of the under-developed lands in relation to the lack of balance in their diets.

3. What is a deficiency disease?

DISCUSSION TOPICS

1. Discuss the underlying problems related to the 'litany of hunger' quoted at the beginning of this chapter.

2. 'Everywhere prices rise and hunger sits at the hearth of millions of people. Here is a match to light the flame of war. The most pressing problem for the greater part of mankind is neither war, nor communism, nor the cost of living, nor taxes; it is hunger. This is because hunger is at the same time the effect and the cause of the poverty and suffering which afflict 1,500 million human beings.'

Fr Noel Drogst in his book *The Challenge of Hunger*. Discuss this quotation.

6: THE FOOD RACE

We expect to have over 6,000 millions of people in the world in A.D. 2000. If each person is to have sufficient good quality food to eat the world's food supplies must be *trebled*. Considerable problems will arise if this target cannot be achieved. Hungry men are a dead weight on any economy and progress can be cut back at the roots. If the nations of the world are to co-exist peacefully the next generation must solve this problem.

Can the world's food supplies increase three fold by the turn of the century?

THE PROBLEM

Agriculture is not only the livelihood of three-quarters of the world's population, it is a way of life; and to change the way of life of most of the world's peoples within a generation is no small task. That the earth is capable of carrying people in far greater numbers than exist today is readily accepted by most experts, but time is the governing factor in the race for food.

The example of Japan is often used to prove the point. With a population approaching 100 millions, averaging 635 persons per square mile, the Japanese survive off only 15 per cent of the land area; the rest is sub-marginal and unfit for cultivation by existing agricultural techniques. To support a world population of 8,000 to 10,000 millions the Japanese level of efficiency would have to be spread throughout the whole of Asia and the rest of the world's agricultural area would have to be increased by 50 per cent and adopt agricultural techniques equivalent in efficiency to those of Western Europe today.* By A.D. 2000 we will need less than this estimate but it gives some idea of the gargantuan task ahead.

* Bonner, J., *The Upper Limits of Crop Yield, 1962.*

It is not so much the 6,000 or 7,000 millions that is so fright-
ening but the fact that this number will probably be reached
by the turn of the century.

A major drawback is that three out of every four human
beings live *on* the land whereas experience shows that more
people can be fed *off* the land. Three-quarters of a million
agricultural workers in Britain feed 32 million fellow country-
men, a ratio of one farm worker to 40 other workers. Mechanization of farming, of course, has brought about this specialization. But of the 11 million farm tractors in use in the world
only about one million are found outside Europe, U.S.S.R.
and North America. Muscle power is wasteful in the race for
food production, although the vast number of subsistence-
level peasants in the world have time on their hands. Considerable, but gradual, progress in mechanization (see page
72), coupled with the expansion of agricultural lands, is
necessarily concurrent with the full utilization of available
manpower.

FOOD TARGETS FOR A.D. 2000

It is evident that not only has the quantity of food to be increased but the quality has to be improved as well, especially
in the increased provision of animal proteins. Moreover, in
considering the food race, attempts must be made to remove
the present disparity in food supplies between developed and
underdeveloped lands. The target is the Food and Agriculture
Organization's food requirement level considered necessary
for the well-being of people in technologically advanced
countries today. Two-thousand six-hundred calories per day
and around 80 grammes of daily protein, of which a half
should be of animal origin, should be the aim.

Reference to Figs. 14 and 15 shows that the various regions
will experience differing problems in interpreting and

achieving this target. Africa is not far short of the calorie level but requires a daily increase of 30 grammes of animal protein to redress the balance. The Far East is in a much worse position for not only is an increase of some 500 calories daily per head required but the animal protein level needs increasing by some 30 grammes. Latin America will be less hard pressed; 16 grammes of extra animal protein will suffice in the tropical areas and the calorie level only needs raising a little.

These are massive requirements and, of course, they cannot be achieved immediately. If they are to be realized, however, a tremendous surge in agricultural productivity is required at once, not only to bridge the present nutritional gap but to cater for the progressive increase in numbers of people. Fig. 16

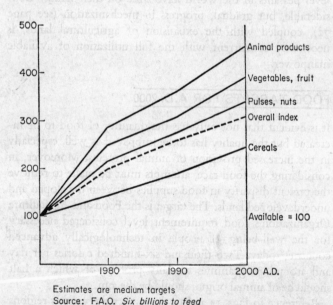

Estimates are medium targets
Source: F.A.O. *Six billions to feed*

Fig. 16. Main Food Supplies required by A.D. 2000.

illustrates the progress required in the underdeveloped countries of the world. (Groups 1 and 4, pages 10 & 11.)

Particular attention must be paid to improving the quality of food and the graph indicates the tremendous spurt required in the protein-rich animal and vegetable commodities compared with the required production of cereals, though an increase of some 150 per cent of the latter will be no easy task. In terms of agricultural productivity the world food output must increase by $3\frac{1}{2}$ per cent per annum to 1980 and 2 per cent per annum thereafter to achieve the required overall increase. On the basis of present supplies this means increases of 50 per cent by 1970, 120 per cent by 1980, 160 per cent by 1990 and, with a massive surge, a 200 per cent increase by A.D. 2000 when the world will require three times its present food supplies.

In using figures of this magnitude it is so easy to consider man as a mere statistic. When we make glib references to intakes per head we should bear in mind that there is a tongue to taste the intake and a stomach to digest it. Ignore these considerations and the man may still go hungry even though food is available. Although food preferences may gradually change, any significant differences between now and A.D. 2000 must be ignored. Half the peoples of the world will not change their eating habits within a generation. Can you imagine the conservative British willingly trading their eggs and bacon or bread and cheese for a monotonous diet of rice and buffalo milk clarified to a sickly oil (*ghee*)? The figures quoted, then, refer to existing dietary preferences.

To maintain these personal tastes cereal production will have to increase by 50 per cent by 1980, nearly 100 per cent by 1990 and almost 150 per cent by 2000. Animal protein products require intensive development with a 350 per cent increase by the turn of the century with vegetable and fruit production trailing significantly in the wake at almost a 300 per cent increase.

The overall requirement is for the world's total food supplies to double by 1980 and treble by the year 2000 to feed a doubled population adequately.

CAN THE FOOD TARGETS BE ACHIEVED BY A.D. 2000?

The immediate requirements of an average annual increase in food supplies of $3\frac{1}{2}$ per cent by 1980 is higher than the 2·7 per cent average increase for the last six years in under-developed countries. In fact the F.A.O. reports* that, per head of population, this increase has only just kept pace with the growth of population without improving either the quality or quantity of food. Fig. 17 illustrates this relative lack of progress.

Appendix 3 (page 108) showing the world's (excluding Mainland China) production of main agricultural commodities details this sad tale of the slow growth of agricultural production relative to population. *Over the past twenty-five years* (pre-war compared with the 1963–4 estimates) the increase for the best outputs in grains does not reach 100 per cent. Fruits and sugar straddle the 100 per cent increase level. Milk has failed to double in output whilst meat and eggs have just topped a 100 per cent increase. This pace is too slow and unless it quickens to a considerable extent a trebled production of today's supplies by A.D. 2000 may be an unrealized target, for the turn of the century is nearer than we think.

Fig. 17 indicates, also, the underdeveloped areas of the Far East, Latin America and Africa. What are their prospects?

The Far East. With the present population of 1,500 millions expected to reach 3,870 millions in A.D. 2000, food supplies will have to increase by about 280 per cent without improving the existing level of nutrition. To close the nutritional gap at

* *Source:* United Nations. F.A.O. *The State of Food & Agric. 1964.*

Indices, average 1952/3 – 1956/7 = 100

Fig. 17. Indices of World (Excluding Mainland China) Agricultural Production in Relation to Population Growth.*

Per Caput Production	Pre-War Average	Average 1948/9 1952/3	Average 1953/4 1957/8	Average 1958/9 1962/3	1958/9	1959/60	1960/1	1961/2	1962/3	1963/4
All Agric. Products	95	95	101	106	105	106	105	105	106	106
Food Products Only	94	95	101	106	106	107	107	105	107	106
Latin America	104	98	101	106	105	102	101	100	98	97
Far East	107	94	101	105	103	105	106	106	105	104
Africa	93	97	100	97	98	97	99	94	96	96

Thus, in production per head of population, there is little difference between the 1958-9 position and that in 1963-4 and the nutritional gap remains despite considerable efforts in many parts of the world to increase food production.

* Source: United Nations, F.A.O. The State of Food & Agric. 1964.

least a 350–400 per cent increase is necessary with emphasis on animal proteins. Fig. 17 does not justify any hope of this rate of progress. India's third Five-Year Plan has seen targets slipping away and similar tales of woe are told by other countries. High illiteracy levels, the lack of investment capital and impoverished soils are the basic deterrents to progress. The indices covering pre-war to 1963/4 (Fig. 17) have shown, in fact, a slight regression over a period of twenty-five years which witnessed a population increase of a little over 400 millions. The next twenty-five years may see an additional population load of about 1,500 millions. Indeed, with the best will in the world and the aid of streamlined and effective Plans, the various governments will be hard pressed to maintain even basic subsistence levels. The problem is massive and, on the basis of present progress, possibly incapable of solution by A.D. 2000 without accompanying disaster.

China, the bogey of the statistician, presents a dilemma to Westeners. It is a nation either marching backwards or providing a ray of hope in the general pessimism of overpopulation. This most populous nation on earth has officially shrugged off the fears of overpopulation, abandoned any extensive support for birth control and maintains that food supplies are increasing at a greater rate than population growth. The 'Great Leap Forward' and the establishment of the People's Communes in 1958 coincided with this apparent conformity to Marxism. The Chinese say that from 1949 to 1959, against an annual rate of population increase of 2 per cent, grain production increased by nearly 10 per cent and that industrial production is swelling even more rapidly. Modern agricultural techniques are alleged to be giving greater yields per acre and so, they say, the fear of overpopulation is a myth created by the Western 'imperialists'. These peaceful claims are based, no doubt, on the facts of geography. China is a land of maldistributed people – empty deserts in the

west and teeming deltas in the east. Only a tenth of the
country is cultivated; two-thirds is barren, mountainous and
semi-desert with an average density of less than one person
per square mile compared with a sixth of the country accom-
modating 90 per cent of the population. There is adequate
room for expansion, given irrigation, without spilling into the
rest of Asia or elsewhere. But a large question-mark hangs
over China; right or wrong, true or false, time alone will tell –
and there is little time left. Inadequate and inaccessible
statistics baulk the rest of the world in the search for an answer
which could be the salvation or destruction of her Asian
neighbours.

Latin America. Argentina, Paraguay, and Uruguay will
probably achieve a 150 per cent increase in population by A.D.
2000. The rest of the southern continental states will nearly
treble their populations. To maintain present standards the
tropical areas will require, therefore, a 200 per cent increase in
food to maintain present standards and a 240 per cent increase* to bring nutritional levels up to F.A.O. requirements.
Despite the fears of overpopulation the problem is light compared with that of the Far East. Land and resources could
quite easily cater for the estimated 592 millions at the end of
the century and, given political stability, the granaries of the
River Plate countries could well save the situation in the last
resort. Latin America may see a tempestuous period of development between now and A.D. 2000 but, with its predicted population, it will still be underdeveloped in relation to
the extent of the natural resources available.

Africa. The African peoples are likely to double their numbers and exceed 500 millions by the turn of the century. Such
a relatively small population base, given political stability in
the jealous welter of newly-gained independence, should be
able to feed adequately off the continental resources. Increased

---

* *Source:* F.A.O. United Nations, 6 *Billions To Feed.*

capital investment and technical assistance will be essential to close the nutritional gap – and they are required urgently. Can the new governments settle down quickly, resolve their differences and attack the scourge of deficiency diseases? To maintain the present low level of food supplies a 100 per cent increase is required by the turn of the century and 160 per cent increase (with emphasis on animal proteins) to meet F.A.O. dietary requirements.

SOME QUESTIONS

1. Outline the world's food targets for A.D. 2000.
2. Comment on the problems of meeting the world's food targets in the Far East by A.D. 2000.
3. What is China's apparent attitude to the problem of food and increasing population?

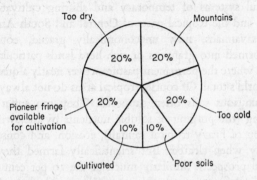

Fig. 18. Utilization of the Earth's Land Area.

In the last chapter, in discussing the prospects of increasing food supplies, it was suggested that the Japanese level of agricultural efficiency would have to spread throughout the whole of Asia and that marginal and even sub-marginal lands, the new pioneer fringes, must be brought under cultivation. In order to achieve this a considerable number of new ideas and methods will have to replace existing systems of agricultural production immediately if the targets for A.D. 2000 are to be realized. That the new pioneer fringes can be pushed outwards is evident from Fig. 18. About a tenth of the world's land area, according to F.A.O. estimates, is cultivated, some two-thirds being devoted to major crops whilst the rest is lying in fallow, temporary pasture or meeting minor crop requirements. Much of the 20 per cent of the pioneer fringe areas is under permanent pastures, often inadequately utilized and the rest, some 70 per cent, is lost to agriculture. How much of this unused land area can be farmed in the immediate future?

Excluding 40 per cent which is mountainous or too cold, the pioneer fringe offers scope for immediate expansion. Some 10 per cent could be utilized for agriculture by ousting the

wasteful systems of temporary and shifting cultivation in
Africa and the tropical parts of Central and South America.
Vast savannahs, now uneconomically grazed, could be
transformed into granaries or rich herd lands particularly in
Africa where the permanent pastures cover nearly a quarter of
the world's total. Of course, tropical areas do not always offer
the luxurious soils often supposed. They can suffer from
leaching (the purging of soluble nutrients by the swift per-
colation of heavy tropical rainfall), erosion, and consequent
sterility when cleared. But scientifically farmed they offer
fruitful prospects. Similarly much of the 10 per cent of the
world's surface covered with poor soils could be brought into
use. At least a half of the dry areas might be irrigated and
brought into the general scheme, giving about a 30 per cent
increase available for cultivation in addition to the existing 10
per cent. Two-fifths of the earth's land surface for potential
crop growth and animal husbandry, compared with the existing tenth, could feed much more than a doubled population
by the turn of the century. But the theoretical possibility
requires translation into practice and problems emerge which
are heightened by the tight time schedule.

DESTROYING THE ROOTS OF PREJUDICE

Governments will have to move swiftly; more far-reaching
efforts are required than are being made at present. The vast
numbers of peasants, often debilitated by malnutrition and
deficiency torpor, will have to be re-educated to a new sense of
purpose. Many traditional methods and religious taboos will
have to be worn down. Outmoded systems of land tenure,
gaping sores in the path of progress, will have to be removed.
New methods of agricultural science cannot be dovetailed
with existing, wasteful practices. The subsequent redistribution of land will hurt; family tradition will be trodden under-

foot but this disintegration will have to be borne if the increased danger of starvation and malnutrition is to be avoided. New techniques of agricultural production will have to be taught and absorbed quickly, going hand in hand with a more forceful attack on illiteracy. Men will have to be persuaded that reform is desirable and imperative.

PRESCRIPTIONS FOR SOIL

Like doctors deciding what kind of a tonic a patient needs, scientists in some American fertilizer companies now 'prescribe' for the requirements of each farm and, if necessary, for each field. Such refinements will not be a practical possibility in any extensive developments in the underdeveloped lands by the turn of the century but a start must be made and new scientific techniques must play a major role. For instance, the Japanese rice yield, with the extensive and intensive use of commercial fertilizer, is 32 cwt. per acre. In India, Burma and Indonesia, where commercial fertilizers are often unheard of and seldom seen, the rice yield averages only 8 cwt. per acre. One Western farmer can feed 30 or 40 people; one Indian farmer is lucky to feed 2 or 3 of his fellows. Such wasteful farming must be swept aside eventually. Fertilizer added to a wheat field can easily multiply the crop fourfold; banish weeds, pests and plant diseases, provide adequate water, improve the quality of the seed and, under ideal conditions, the original miserable yield can be increased tenfold. But to reach such planned perfection organized surveys must assess the potential of the soil profiles. Here the researches of the West can assist the East for no planned agricultural development can succeed without an adequate diagnosis of soil conditions. The extent and type of chemical fertilizer required depends on such information. The natural fertility of overworked tropical soils is often low. Better soil management allowing for crop rotation and the use of fertilizers could increase food output by at least 50 and possibly 100 per cent in most under-developed areas, say the F.A.O. experts. This demands the efficient use of natural fertilizer, the abolition of such practices as using cow dung for fuel in India, and of course, the provision of facilities for the manufacture of fertilizers.

New developments offer constant hope. Researchers are feeding treated oil to chickens and livestock to increase the protein potential. Petroleum mulch sprayed on shifting sand dunes assists stabilization and ultimate cropping. Plastiponics, the science of utilizing foamed-plastic soil, has demonstrated the possibility of retaining moisture in the parched sands of the Middle East. Butyl rubber, used as a lining for irrigation ditches, is reducing the 40 per cent water loss by seepage in dry lands. Far-fetched and impracticable, perhaps, for wide application at this stage; but here are possible pointers to the future developments of the new pioneer fringes.

PLANT BREEDING

Science is enabling man to virtually tailor-make his crops for specific requirements of climate, soils, quality, taste and resistance to disease. Such resources must be tapped. Plant breeders have produced strains which are well adapted to some of the more rigorous conditions of the various pioneer fringes – low winter temperatures, inadequate rainfall and the devastation of wind. Atomic radiation is playing its part in providing a wider range of mutations to assist the breeder in his selection and crossing of strains. So far the underdeveloped areas have received little benefit from these advances in the laboratories of the West and more research will be necessary to produce strains to fit tropical requirements. Money, qualified personnel and the establishment of plant breeding stations are essential.

A half of man's total protein supply comes directly from grains. Indirectly, with a half of this amount being fed to livestock, they underwrite animal proteins. In general, however, grains are probably reaching their limit as a major contributor to protein supplies. The essential need is for more animal protein, for there is a limit to the amount of bulky grain food with which a person can distend his stomach. As calorie suppliers, grains still play the leading role but their development in the pioneer fringe will be in replacing starchy foods (cassava, yams and sweet potatoes) which have a lower calorie content. Grains could be grown to a far greater extent in Africa where, for example, rice could replace in wetter areas the staple starchy roots, providing food habits are sufficiently elastic. But such new introductions must be tailored to suit the soil and bred to produce the highest yield possible. Like all highly bred strains, however, they will be vulnerable to pests and parasites and must be protected accordingly.

PESTS AND PLANT DISEASES

The Food and Agriculture Organization estimates that insect pests consume between a quarter and a third of all the world's crops today. Irrespective of all other measures designed to increase food supplies, the control of pests can make a significant contribution to increased supplies. Moreover, chemical insecticides can be applied by the farmer on the spot. One harvest is sufficient for him to recognize the value of this control; instant education is available. But sometimes, as with the all-consuming locusts which range over wide areas, international co-operation and control is necessary.

Chemical control is cheap compared with the saving in crops. A quarter of Ghana'a cocoa crop was lost in 1951 through the hunger of insect pests. By 1959, with the intensive use of insecticides, the yield had doubled in most areas.

Science has produced many fungicides, insecticides, antibiotics and weed-killers to combat the ravages of pests and
plant diseases but there has been a growing concern about
possible adverse effects of their liberal application and attention has been focused on natural control. Predators of the
insect pests have been introduced occasionally as in the
United Kingdom where experiments are being made with
a virus to eliminate the cabbage white butterfly. Fish in
flooded Eastern rice fields feed off mosquito larvae. Much
of this biological control is in its infancy and could be significant in the food race for, by simply reforming nature's legions,
the control proceeds behind the farmer's back and yields
multiply.

MEN OR MACHINES?

The wooden plough is still used by three out of every four of
the world's farmers; it scratches the earth and is a symbol of
ignorance and inefficiency. Many people advocate revolution-
izing farming in underdeveloped lands by introducing the
tractor, but such measures need careful consideration. Stag-
gered lines of harvesters on the Canadian prairies suit the
situation because men are sprinkled sparsely over vast, level
plains. But the overpopulated lands have a surplus of labour.
Machines would increase the idle pressure and add to social
problems. Whilst men are still readily available machines can
well wait, for although they increase the acreage, they seldom
add to the output per acre. Until the underdeveloped areas
can absorb surplus labour in industrial enterprise, priority
must go to improving existing tools. The wooden plough-
hook needs a steel tip or share; quicker transport than the
plodding ox is required. Any measures which improve the
output per worker are necessary. It has been indicated already
that muscle power is wasteful in the short, sharp race for food

production and if the population pressure becomes too intense in the twenty-first century mechanization may be indispensable. But, for the present, the transition must be handled delicately.

ANIMAL DILEMMA

When a man's social status and wealth are revealed by his head of cattle, irrespective of their well-being or profitability, or where he worships them as part of his creed, allows them to share his hearth but will not, or cannot, feed them, there is little prospect of immediate and successful selective breeding of animals. Tradition and prejudice are obstinate enemies to progress. Better animal husbandry, the reduction of overstocked, underfed herds and the improvement of pastures are necessary but difficult to achieve under these conditions. Scraggy beasts compete with their owners for food rather than providing food – an unfortunate dilemma because animal proteins are in acute short supply in overpopulated lands. Time, again, is the essence of the problem. Wearing down prejudice and belief in order to adjust the number of animals to the carrying capacity of the available pastures will be a long process. When this has been achieved selective breeding will be possible.

Much better results are likely to arise from immediate attention to cattle diseases. Rinderpest, foot and mouth disease and many parasitic infections cut off the supply of animal protein and help to widen the nutritional gap. But work of this nature demands technicians and veterinarians. Here the trained resources of the West can give immediate assistance.

THE PROBLEM OF WATER

Water is as necessary as food and its availability will determine the extent to which existing agricultural areas can expand and how far the pioneer fringes can be opened up. The need for water even gives concern in developed areas. Cries for the conservation of water are heard each summer in various part of Great Britain. In U.S.A. 45 per cent of the water supplies are used for industrial purposes, 45 per cent for agriculture and 10 per cent in households. Water, then, could be a determining factor in the industrialization of underdeveloped lands.

Certainly water is not an inexhaustable resource and the rapid multiplication of population in the future must cause concern. Conservation of existing supplies is the first need. Forty per cent of irrigated water is lost through seepage. Much is lost (and many lives) through pollution. The Ganges, the 'river of life' and a natural sewer, makes life a hazard and death a privilege for those who drink its turgid waters.

Water is also powerfully destructive. The Chinese peasant, living under the shadow of raised levées, is naked to its onslaught. Flood protection and control are necessary and costly. Often such measures require international co-operation where river basins cross frontiers. Integrated, whole-basin development is essential and river boards ignoring national boundaries are required. The basic squabbles between India and Pakistan in the Punjab bear testimony to the lack of foresight in mutual river control.

The dry lands of the pioneer fringes require special attention. Hydrogeologic mapping may seek out unknown aquifers which will bring the waters of life to many desert and semi-desert areas thus allowing population to spread. The Saharan aquifer adequately tapped could well transform this landscape into a cultivated garden.

But possibly the greatest source of new water supplies lies in the sea, provided the salt content can be removed. Many nations, particularly U.S.A., have given considerable attention to the various possibilities of freezing, electrical removal or a complicated system of distillation. All these methods are costly in the power they need and so the poor, underdeveloped areas may be denied their use until a cheap and effective solar process is invented. The need for converting sea water has been recognized in high places. In 1950, President Truman invited Congress 'to find ways of de-mineralizing salt waters'. And in 1961 President Kennedy crystallized the thoughts of many people in stating:

'No programme for supplying water holds a more important place – in the long run – (not only in regard to our own scarcity but also to meet the needs of the arid regions of the entire world) than that leading to a successful conclusion of our research to perfect an efficient and economic method of converting the vast, natural wealth of our oceans into water for domestic and industrial use. A success in this order would put an end to the bitter conflicts that set neighbours, provinces and nations against one another, and would bring hope to millions of individuals who, throughout their life, have suffered from lack of water and have been unable to profit from the physical and economic benefits that this immense ocean, which touches their arid regions, could have brought them.'

Once water is available, it must be controlled and used to the best advantage. That irrigation can transform the desert soils is seen in West Pakistan, which would not have existed as a state today if the irrigation programme initiated by the British at the end of the last century had not transformed the Punjab into a granary. Perhaps one of the most striking aspects of the agricultural development of many tropical areas in this century has been the increasing extent to which irrigation has been achieved. But only 15 per cent of cultivated land in the world today depends on irrigation. To feed the increased population of the future much more must be done – and irrigated water is costly.

MARINE AGRICULTURE

Increased fish supplies could probably fill the animal protein gap in the world if the problems of taste, processing and transportation could be overcome. At present, fish account for only some 3 per cent of the animal protein eaten in the world. Fig. 19 shows that the peoples of the Far East consume a little over a third of the world supplies.

Fig. 19. Estimated World Catch of Fish, Crustaceans and Molluscs.*

Area	1938	Average 1948/52	1963
W. Europe	5·52	6·24	8·3
E. Europe & U.S.S.R.	1·62	1·94	4·5
N. America	3·11	3·50	4·0
Oceania	0·09	0·09	0·1
Latin America	0·28	0·60	8·7
Far East	9·44	7·80	17·3
Near East	0·31	0·35	0·5
Africa	0·47	1·06	2·6
World Total	20·84	21·58	46·0

(Figures in million metric tons, live weight.)

* Source: United Nations. F.A.O. The State of Food & Agriculture 1964.

The Far East supplies could well be increased from the plentiful waters sweeping round the south-eastern coasts for only an estimated 30 per cent of the world's catch comes from tropical waters. There is no lack of fish in warmer waters; they merely need catching.

When we remember that seven-tenths of the world's surface is covered by sea water it is surprising that relatively little attention has been paid to its harvest. Certainly with the increasing pressure on land many men would do well to face seawards. Occasional examples illustrate the vast potential; the Japanese relieved, to a certain extent, their food problem by increasing their annual catch from 2 million metric tons in 1945 to 6·7 million metric tons in 1961. There is no immediate fear of depleting the oceans' resources for the F.A.O. estimates that two and a half times more fish could be caught without endangering future supplies.

The problem is that man is still in the primitive hunting stage in catching fish. For extensive exploitation he needs to farm fish as he does his land animals. Marine agriculture needs the impetus which the agricultural revolution had on land – but much more quickly. Vast stretches of sunlit seas could be used as algae farms supplying valuable protein which could be fed to fenced fish, land animals or even humans if they could acquire the taste . . . the possibilities are limitless providing capital, effort and will are forthcoming.

CONCLUSION

This panorama of possible changes in agricultural production to ensure a tripled food supply by A.D. 2000 has emphasized many possibilities and problems. There is no doubt that 6,000 to 7,000 million souls can be catered for. Many resources and much technical knowledge have to be unearthed and shared. But even more is required; improved transport facilities, adequate handling and processing techniques must be brought to the underdeveloped lands. Assured markets, stable prices; the regular supply of fertilizers, accessible advisory services and equipment must all play complementary roles in the short, sharp race for food.

But the underdeveloped lands are poor and the richer nations are more concerned with political gambits for power. It must be concluded regrettably that all these changes seem unlikely to be achieved, within the next thirty years, to feed a doubled world population. Whilst the overpopulated countries maintain their high rate of fertility the race for the food targets of A.D. 2000 is likely to be lost.

SOME QUESTIONS

1. What are the 'new pioneer fringes'?
2. Explain the 'animal dilemma'.
3. Consider the main lines of advance along which the underdeveloped countries might endeavour to get *quick* results in improving the quantity and quality of their food supplies.

DISCUSSION TOPICS

1. Discuss the problem of 'men versus machines' in underdeveloped areas.
2. Danger to the world's future food supplies springs not so much from a lack of nature's gifts or human resources as from indifference, apathy and lack of action.
     Discuss this statement.
3. The author concludes that, in the short space of time available, man is likely to lose the food race. Do you agree?

8: INDUSTRIALIZATION: DRAWING PEOPLE OFF THE LAND

THE NEED FOR INDUSTRY—AND TIME

As an antidote for relieving the increasing pressure of population in the rural areas of underdeveloped lands, many people advocate the establishment of industry. Where natural resources and conditions are suitable, industry will give balance to the economy and assist in raising the standard of living which, ultimately, may induce people to voluntarily restrict population growth on Western lines. Nehru recognized that 'no country, unless it has a developed industry, can enjoy independence'. No doubt he had in mind the widening gap between the £800 annual income per head in U.S.A. compared with the £25 per head in his own country. Poverty-stricken nations watch the industrial nations growing richer on the strength of one or two centuries of experience and prestige whilst they remain impoverished. Often the pressure of population panics them into plans to ape this development – and time is their enemy, even allowing for the short-cuts of Western aid and 'know-how'.

That industry will be beneficial in the long run is hardly in dispute. It is the means of establishing it which give rise to arguments, for industrialization has profound and far-reaching effects. It alters man's economic status and can redirect his cultural and social development. Britian's transition from an agricultural to an industrial economy provided two centuries of gradual acclimatization for succeeding generations. Think how much more striking the changes must seem when industrialization comes suddenly to a country. Much controversy surrounds the various effects of industrialization, as we shall see.

HAND IN HAND DEVELOPMENT

Some want instant industry in underdeveloped lands; others, in fear of food shortages, would take agriculture as their industry. The truth is that both must go hand in hand where possible; the one stimulates the other. Industry begets an urban population which can pay for its food. The lure of cash stimulates the farmers to meet this demand and the seeds of the transition from subsistence farming to commercial farming are sown. Three-quarters of the food produced in the average Indian village is consumed on the spot and little of the rest leaves the immediate locality. If the new industrial workers, in relieving the pressure on the land, cannot be fed then industry cannot start.

Underdeveloped countries will never be independent if they are forced to import regularly all the commercial fertilizers, steel and other necessities for respectable independence. In the beginning industrialization will throw them into debt but the interest will be relieved to a certain extent by the stimulus given to agriculture. And to complete the cycle, the farmers will be in a better position to buy the products of the industry they feed.

RETARDING FACTORS IN THE DEVELOPMENT OF INDUSTRY

Men and money are the main obstacles to industrial development in overpopulated countries. *Too many men* prevent the accumulation of money within these impoverished nations. The balance of payments for imports and exports is always in a precarious state and even when capital is begged, borrowed or saved and machines and equipment installed, *too few men* adequately trained in the skills of industry are available to operate and maintain it. Once industry is established the impetus for training and education is given. Engineering specifications have to be read and understood; safety regulations require interpretation. Even easily acquired semi-skills need the base of education for their extensive absorption by the mass of the people – and the dividends for investment in education are not immediate. Moreover, industry needs the support of general education to develop specialized technical training schemes. And to guide and develop industrialization, managers and industrial leaders are required. Such men are born of experience and they are at a premium in underdeveloped countries. To span the years until an efficient, native managerial class arises, the trained manpower of the developed countries must be used – but only to bridge the waiting period of education and experience.

Time, again, is the retarding factor in getting the right men and adequate funds for the development of industry.

POLITICS AND PLANNING

Planning is essential if industry and agriculture are to go hand in hand and often, in seeking the support of uncommitted, emergent nations, capitalist and socialist countries push their planning systems with aid and advice attached to political strings. Socialist countries preach complete public ownership and state control in all aspects of planning whereas capitalism allows the freedom of private enterprise within a planned programme. Whichever system is adopted, however, account must be taken of the inter-relationships of all aspects of the environment. There is no master blueprint to satisfy the needs of all underdeveloped countries. Each plan must be tailored to suit the country concerned. Geographical location, climate, the availability of and prospects for communications, resources and power, and man in all aspects of his capabilities and failings must be borne in mind. The need to decentralize industry is important. The tendency, to be discussed later, for people to swell the already swollen main cities presents serious social problems. New towns as secondary industrial centres are needed to give a balanced network of urban communities.

Many underdeveloped countries have recognized the need for these requirements and have attempted to regulate their development by Five- and Ten-Year, or other, Plans. But one common thread is evident. Few Plans meet their targets on time. With increasing population pressure such countries are seldom better off at the end than at the start.

THE LOCATION OF INDUSTRY

Planning is essential but slow in application. In Great Britain the Industrial Revolution was conceived from local initiative and industry sprawled its arbitrary way through the land. Often the factors responsible for the original development of the industry have disappeared but it is carried along by geographical momentum. Which modern planner would ever design a Sheffield today, hemmed in by Pennine Hills, distant from its Swedish ore and having outgrown and abandoned the local resources? In developing their industrial revolution, the underdeveloped countries have the benefit of two hundred years of such Western experience. In the siting of industry they must look beyond the short-term advantages of natural location. In the long run it may be unwise to set up an iron and steel industry because local ore is available if the regional or national pattern is marred. And once an industry is established it takes economic and social roots which are difficult to sever.

The pursuit of industry should be the pursuit of human

happiness and underdeveloped countries need to stem the flow of people to the major cities which are developing a fringe of bulging shanty towns. People need spreading wider by the injection of industry into stagnant smaller towns. New towns can bleed this cancerous population growth of the major cities. Thus the planning of industrial location can be a major factor in this necessary redistribution of population. Natural location, except for the immediate exploitation of resources such as the extraction of minerals, is seldom in fashion today. Transmitted hydro-electric power and improved communications now allow the artificial siting of industry on a scale which would have been impossible at the start of the Industrial Revolution in Europe. The underdeveloped countries should take advantage of this and plan the development of industry to cope, not with their present population distribution, but with at least a doubled population load within the next thirty years.

Such an artificial network of industrial units can only exist with an efficient system of linking transport, and the underdeveloped lands are ill-equipped in this respect. The ox-cart clings tenaciously to its miserable status in an Asia which houses over half the world's population and three per cent of its motor vehicles. In major industrial planning these poor countries can benefit from the experience of the West for transport costs account for, on average, about a third of the costs of industrial production. Efficient planning now will save money in the future. Every plan, every road, every railway devised now must look at the turn of the century and have as its reference at least a doubled population potential. Time is short; plans have the habit of clinging to the drawing board for a long time and require even longer for translation on the ground.

WHAT KIND OF INDUSTRY?

Opionions differ on the types of industry which can be established in underdeveloped areas. Some would have the pattern of the West transferred completely. Others shun this suggestion; they are conscious of the leap over the centuries and are more practical in their approach. They cannot envisage the sophisticated industrial pattern of the West merging easily into the background of the East. They prefer the more practical approach of working from the known to the unknown in establishing industries which require many hands rather than much capital. Light manufacturing industries present a smaller step in the transition from the traditional handicrafts of cottage industries. Certainly they will be established much quicker and will absorb more labour and less capital than heavy industry. On the other hand, heavy industry attracts many secondary industries which are required to give balance to the industrial scene.

In general most experts seem to support, initially, the establishment of light industry to be followed, when time, capital and circumstances permit, by heavy industry. For example, the chronic malnutrition of the East could well be reduced by light industries preserving and processing foodstuffs. Once the stimulus has been given the engineering industry could be extended to underwrite the needs of agriculture in the production of farm machinery and implements. The production of fertilizers would take pride of place in any programme to stimulate agricultural output and lessen the dependence on imported material.

Iron and steel, the buttress of most industrialized economies, may well be a late starter in underdeveloped lands. This industry is costly to establish, will work below capacity for the first ten years, requires trained personnel and, relative to cost, absorbs little labour. Most underdeveloped lands can find the raw materials but not the money or men. The 'know-how' is available from abroad; hydro-electric power is often accessible. But heavy industry consumes time. It will be essential for the twenty-first century development of the East but is unlikely to be a real benefit before the end of the twentieth century.

SWOLLEN CITIES

There is no doubt that industrial planning has a major rôle to play in halting the drift to the cities which cannot absorb the exodus from the countryside. In particular, it is the major cities which are receiving the onslaught – a trend which is found in most underdeveloped countries. One in every five Latin Americans lives in a city of over 100,000 inhabitants. A third of the world's large city populations (over 100,000 inhabitants) are found in Asia. Seven out of every ten Israelis live in large towns. This pattern of the swelling of the large towns is being increasingly repeated in most of the emergent and underdeveloped lands. Of course, the rural areas can breathe with relief but the smaller towns are becoming eddies in economic backwaters whilst the main city concentrations have insufficient industry to absorb the influx.

If the swelling of the major cities is not eased, the turn of the century may see the urban populations increased from the present 25 per cent to 50 per cent of the total world population, based on present trends. And as the main population increases will be in the East, its major cities could become festering, unclean sores of humanity. These people in relieving the burden of country areas are merely exchanging rural poverty for urban misery. It is estimated that a third of the inhabitants of major cities in underdeveloped lands crowd into crude, shanty shelters with no water, sewers or other services. Disease is rife – the product of over-urbanization which in turn arises from rural overpopulation. The urban labour market is flooded and wages drop. Men cut each other's throats for work. Family unity is broken; delinquency and crime increase; the social fabric tears.

Industrialization can assist in reversing this trend by flushing the backwaters of smaller towns and giving balance to urban development. Concurrently, and ideally, the expansion of agriculture in the areas surrounding the new industrial developments will provide the food. The factory will stimulate the field and the first link in the chain of economic progress will have been forged.

AID AND HINDSIGHT

In the underdeveloped nations' industrial leap across the centuries the assistance of the richer nations is essential. But pushing a concertinaed industrial revolution over a few decades will be an impossible task; the mass of planning and work to be done, harassed by an ever-increasing population, is unlikely to be achieved by the turn of the century. That industry needs to be established is beyond doubt and the developed nations can smooth the path. In this respect the poorer nations have one advantage; hindsight. With the aid of the richer nations they can avoid many of the mistakes of the infancy of the Industrial Revolution in the West, providing they plan and profit by the advice.

SOME QUESTIONS

1. Explain the need for industry in underdeveloped lands.
2. How can industry and agriculture play complementary rôles in the development of eastern Asia?
3. Explain recent ideas in development plans for overpopulated countries.

DISCUSSION TOPICS

1. Discuss the factors which may limit the development of industry in underdeveloped countries in the next few decades.

2. Discuss the social problems associated with the rush to the cities in overpopulated countries.

3. *Industry and Time*. Discuss the prospects for A.D. 2000.

9: THE THIRD FREEDOM

'... Four essential freedoms. The first is freedom of speech ... the second is freedom of every person to worship God in his own way. *The third is freedom from want* ... the fourth is freedom from fear.'

FRANKLIN D. ROOSEVELT, 1941

How far distant is the realization of the Third Freedom? According to United Nations calculations, based on present progress in relation to predicted population increases, it could take up to 200 years before living standards in underdeveloped countries are able to catch up with those in western Europe today. There are so many questionable variables in such a prediction that it is possibly valueless. Nevertheless, it may be nearer the truth than any suggestion that the problem of want will be solved by the turn of the century.

Much will depend on the extent to which the underdeveloped countries are able to help themselves and curb their natural rates of increase. But the speed of achieving the Third Freedom will depend on the amount of aid which flows from the richer to the poorer nations. The massive problems of capital, technical assistance, illiteracy and social change will have to be overcome as quickly as possible, for the aid from the richer nations must be construed as 'first aid' only; it cannot be accepted as part of an established pattern. 'Development assistance' is a better term for the ultimate aim is that each nation should be able to solve its own problems by its own effort. In fact the sixties have been designated the *Development Decade* by the United Nations to emphasize the urgency of the problem and to persuade rich and poor to meet the challenge. The goal of the *Decade* is to ensure that by 1970 the productivity of the poor nations will be increasing by 5 per cent per annum – a rate sufficient to break through the population increase barrier. To achieve this, each developed nation would have to contribute at least one per cent of its national income to overseas development. Much as we are doing in this direction, Britain is giving only 0·6 per cent for this purpose at present.

Of course, there are those who say that we cannot afford it, that we are in no way responsible for the irresponsible breeding of the poorer peoples. Others would willingly pay up in the hope that a better standard of living will reduce the pressure of numbers and the possibility of a world calamity based on want. Yet others are aghast at the £35,000 millions annual world defence budget; use this for development assistance, they say. Whatever the arguments, the targets for the *Development Decade* are unlikely to be achieved by 1970 at the present rate of progress. Unless the causes of the poverty of the underdeveloped countries are removed, no solution is possible. A United Nations Conference on Trade and Development, held in 1964 at Geneva, tackled this problem. For the first time the *77 Bloc*, seventy-seven poor, underdeveloped nations represented at the conference, expressed their combined determination to tackle the problem whilst the richer nations promised to give one per cent of their national income for the development of the *77 Bloc*. Perhaps this renewed impetus may make the targets of the *Development Decade* more realistic.

WHAT KIND OF AID?

Aid has many guises. It can come as straight grants often reflecting the generosity of the donor and sometimes the humility of the recipient. But modern aid is not intended as charity; it should be development assistance with no political ties. Loans are often thought to be more dignified and not so politically suspect, but they demand repayment with interest at a time when the borrower requires this money for reinvestment in the development of his own country. Material help in the form of food surpluses, gifts of equipment and clothing are stop-gap measures which can allow development programmes to start unharried.

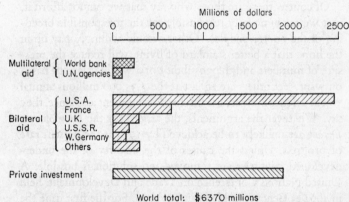

Fig. 20. Capital Assistance for Underdeveloped Countries.

Fig. 20 indicates the three main types of capital aid.

MULTILATERAL AID

This type of aid is ideally the best insofar as it is normally free from the charge of political favour. But it represents little more than 5 per cent of the total capital aid because donors in the international scene rarely prefer anonymity. Consequently the United Nations Organization contributes less than 2 per cent of the capital aid, but more than makes up for this in the variety of its advice and assistance. A *Special Fund* finances investigations into suggested development schemes. The *Technical Assistance Board* spreads its personnel far and wide as do those of the various U.N. agencies. The *World Health*

Organization fights disease and endeavours to improve the mental and physical health of people everywhere. UNESCO fights illiteracy. The *United Nations Children's Fund* (UNICEF), originally formed to meet the emergency needs of European children after the war, now caters for the world and assists in feeding schemes for some 55 millions of children and mothers each year. The *Food and Agriculture Organization*, whose statistics have been liberally quoted in this book, is concerned with all aspects of food production and the raising of living standards together with the provision of technical advice and assistance to this end.

BILATERAL AID

This is direct government-to-government aid and is by far the biggest source in the world. Fig. 20 shows how the U.S.A. contributes nearly two-thirds of the total with France a significant second and U.K. a much smaller third. U.S.S.R., of course, is spending money on expansion within her own borders, although more external assistance has been given since the end of the Stalin régime, e.g. the Aswan High Dam in Egypt.

The drawback to bilateral aid is that it smacks of political favour and, as such, can undermine the free political development of the receiving nation. The political grouping of the world's population today is shown by Fig. 21.

Without doubt, and with due respect to the good intentions of American aid, 'Possibility 2' is the one which pushes their aid so much in advance of that of other nations. It explains, for example, why Taiwan (Formosa), the last island stronghold of Nationalist China, received, in 1960, $105 million for a population of 11 millions compared with the $450 million of aid to India with its 450 millions. Russian aid to Cuba and American retaliation brought the world to the brink of war.

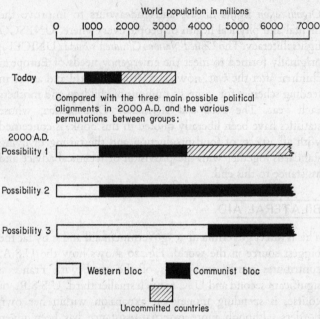

Fig. 21. Population and Power Politics.

South Vietnam figured highly in the American aid programme in 1966 whilst North Vietnam had Communist support. Of the total American bilateral foreign aid about a third is devoted to direct military assistance to other countries. The extent to which military considerations, economic growth and self-help are often related in bilateral aid is seen in President Johnson's message to the U.S.A. Congress on *The State of the Union 1965*.

'. . . Military security in the developing world will not be sufficient in our purposes unless the ordinary people begin to feel some improvement in their lives and see ahead to a time when their children can live in decency. It follows that economic growth in these regions means as much to our security as their military strength. That is an important reason why the United States has taken the lead during the past few years in organizing, on an international basis, a programme of development assistance.

'They need to undertake sound measures of self-help – to mobilize their own resources, eliminate waste, and do what they can to meet their own needs. And they need to avoid spending their resources on unnecessary armaments and foreign adventures. Our aid can contribute to their economic and social progress only if it can be provided within a framework of constructive and sensible policies and programmes. Fortunately, more of the developing countries recognize the relationship between the wise use of their own resources and the effectiveness and availability of external aid.

'It is a cardinal principle of U.S. policy that development assistance will go to countries which have undertaken effective programmes of self-help and are, therefore, able to make good use of aid. With development assistance we seek to help countries reach, as rapidly as possible, the point at which further progress is possible without external aid.'

Despite political undercurrents, however, bilateral aid has done much to launch development programmes in many of the poorer countries.

PRIVATE INVESTMENT

Private investment makes a significant contribution, about a third, to the annual inflow of capital to underdeveloped lands. As with bilateral aid it is often suspect; exploitation of the worst colonial type is often feared and sometimes evident, but private funds have done a great deal in developing the resources of backward countries. The Middle East would have been nothing without oil; Malaya, rubber and tin are inseparable . . . and there are many more examples. With adequate safeguards at government level, there is no reason why private investment should not continue to play a significan part in the development of poor countries. Similarly the various voluntary agencies such as *Oxfam* and religious organizations, although less spectacular in donating hard cash, have a significant part to play in the mobilization of public goodwill in the donor countries and the example they set in the recipient nations of the need for self-help.

TRADE AS AID

Trade is a much more dignified way of acquiring money for development. The income from exports of the under-developed lands is about ten times that from overseas aid and the richer nations could do a great deal to foster this spirit of enterprise; to encourage these infant lands to establish the pattern of earning their aid and sharing, more equitably, in the fruits of trade.

Much of what they export, mainly farm produce such as coffee, tea, bananas, cocoa and vegetable oils, is sold to the richer nations. As production has grown to meet the increased demands of the West, prices have dropped on the principle of 'the bigger the crop, the lower the price'. Sometimes native farmers have burned excess crops to maintain price levels. Such market conditions discourage the poorer nations from spending money on improved farming methods to grow more produce which will earn less. Paradoxically, the trade gains of the West and the losses suffered by the underdeveloped nations approximate to the amount of aid given by the West; overseas aid is often termed 'conscience money'!

It might be better if developed countries, instead of giving direct bilateral aid, encouraged the sale of tropical products in temperate lands by reducing import taxes and guaranteeing prices. Not only would the developing nations have the dignity and satisfaction of earning their own living by the stimulation of international trade but the main political pressures might be released.

QUOTATIONS FOR DISCUSSION TOPICS

1. 'The conscience of mankind is a diffuse kind of vapour which only rarely condenses into working steam' – Arthur Koestler.

Comment on this statement in relation to the organization of voluntary aid to underdeveloped countries.

2. 'Hunger is the world's greatest politician' – Lord Boyd Orr.

3. 'We must all admire the way in which the peoples of those (the less-developed) countries have responded to this challenge with vigour and determination, and it is our privilege in the West – and, I would say, our duty – to help them with our capital and our skills. We are not seeking political advantage or narrow commercial benefits when we give help, nor do we limit our aid to large-scale projects of the maximum advertising value. We give our help because we want these countries to be strong and prosperous, because that is right in itself and because we think that the prosperity of all is for the good of all. We are not jealous of the assistance given by other governments. The world's requirements are so great that there is ample room – indeed there is an urgent need – for disinterested help by all' – Harold Macmillan.

10: WORD CONTROL AND BIRTH CONTROL

Previous chapters have outlined the extent of the population problem. The explosive statistics have been examined and there is every reason to believe that the prediction of a doubled population by A.D. 2000 will materialize if present trends continue. Possible solutions have been considered in the form of improved and extended land use, industrialization and development assistance in all its aspects. All are capable of easing the pressure of population and banishing hunger and malnutrition. That the earth can carry adequately a doubled, or even trebled, population – *given time* – is accepted by most experts. But time, or rather population, does not wait for resources to increase, for the people of the underdeveloped lands are multiplying at a greater rate than their food supplies. Once this basic fact is recognized, the answer may well seem simple. If a plugged wash-basin is being filled at a greater rate than the overflow can take and the water escapes on to the floor, do we seize our mops and engage in a relentless fight against the cascade? Do we rush for buckets to contain the flow? Common sense suggests that we restrict the supply; we turn off the tap.

So with the flow of people; the peasants of the underdeveloped lands need the common sense to restrict their increase and the realization that birth control can achieve this. But there are many divided opinions on the acceptance of birth control for it is an extremely delicate subject. Nevertheless, allowing for the various ethical arguments to be discussed later, it would appear that there is no choice. Birth control is the only alternative to suffocation. The anti-birth-controllers have been slow to give ground and there is still no general acceptance. But the theoretical debates in the

West about the rights and wrongs of birth control are in any case no comfort to the poor woman in her miserable hovel who has had ten children in as many years because she knows that only three or four will survive – or is it that only three or four survive because she has had ten children? Who knows the motivations in the mind of such a mother? Perhaps she cannot make any logical assessment of her problem; perhaps she never thinks of it as a problem. It is the lot of everyone around; it is normal.

To clear away this lack of understanding, education and birth control are the twin salvations. Education is a slow form of investment and birth control, although readily applied, depends on understanding through education – and twin dilemmas are encountered.

LITERACY AND ILLUSION

Approximate illiteracy rates, expressed as a percentage of total population for various countries, are:

United Kingdom, W. Germany, Denmark, New Zealand (1); Japan (2); U.S.A., France (3); U.S.S.R. (5); Italy (10); Chile (20); Mexico, Ceylon (35); Brazil (50); Guatemala (70); Egypt, Ghana (75); India, Pakistan, Indonesia (80).

These figures give some idea of the burden of illiteracy in the underdeveloped countries. Illiteracy implies not only the inability to read and write but the allied world of superstition, ignorance and the lack of incentive to get out of that world. This is the lot of nearly half the world's peoples – the hungry, poverty-stricken ones. Illiteracy is the ally of hunger because superstition and ignorance do nothing to combat the deficiency diseases which result from it.

The development programme of any country requires the co-operation of the mass of the people for it involves not only the training of skilled technicians but the sweeping away of patterns of social behaviour which bar progress. A developing country needs a positive and enlightened attitude in all its peoples towards progress and change. Teaching people to simply read and write will not achieve this, for the unintelligent reading of books and newspapers is near-illiteracy. The spread of primary education, of course, is essential; but on this must be built a desire for a deeper involvement in the social and economic development of the country. Only from such a base can a nation heave itself from the morass of poverty. Complete education of this type is a lengthy process. Its fruits will not be evident immediately and time, as with all other aspects of the population problem, is the enemy. But a greater impetus must be given to education than exists at present, for the whole development of the illiterate world cannot grow from ill-equipped classes under the shade of local banyan trees.

Isolated spurts of education produce their problems. Those people who do escape from the mesh of ignorance in the underdeveloped lands may become disillusioned. They are impatient of the poverty which surrounds them; they look for instant relief. Power politics can draw them and they often become pawns in the education race between East and West. Much of the instability of the newly emerged nations stems from the impatience of such angry young men. In the long run their impatience may mar the development of the country they wish to serve.

TO BREED OR NOT TO BREED?

The earlier chapters of this book emphasized that the increased population of the underdeveloped countries is caused by the decline in death rates in relation to relatively stable birth rates. This pressure could be eased by asking these prolific peoples to produce fewer children, that is to plan their families by adopting methods of birth control. Otherwise an increasing number of people will go hungry. Overcrowding will breed massive frustrations and if suffocation does not snuff out the human race, annihilation by a big bang could result. Indifference to such warnings is a major problem; too many people regard suggestions that the world is building its funeral pyre with its birth certificates as mere alarmist gimmickry.

WHAT IS BIRTH CONTROL?

The term 'birth control' implies any deliberate practice which prevents conception. There are both artificial and natural methods but no completely safe technique is known. To some the practice is objectionable on moral and religious grounds and, for the poorer people of the world, artificial methods are often too dear and natural methods too difficult to understand. The 'safe' period involves the complicated recognition of the precise time of ovulation (after which conception is likely to occur) in the woman's menstrual cycle. The Indian government, after extensive research, found that this method proved too much for the understanding of peasant women. How can a woman who cannot count, reckon the days to the 'safe' period? The 'pill', the new oral contraceptive, is still in its infancy. Too little is known of any long-term side-effects at present for its use to be universally supported. If continued research proves it to be safe and it can be produced cheaply, it would be the answer to the population problem in the underdeveloped areas. Sterilization and abortion also come within the meaning of the term although to most people they are morally objectionable except under medical advice. The former is an irretrievable decision and the latter can be dangerous to the health of the mother and, as such, they are negative forms of birth control as opposed to positive family planning. Certainly Japan had startling and effective results with legalized abortion (see page 42) in reducing her rate of increase within a very short space of time. But the Japanese government is now advocating positive birth control techniques having established the atmosphere for control.

A PRACTICAL POINT OF VIEW

It is obvious that in countries where women are hungry and malnourished, they are in no fit state to bear large numbers of children. Death is often a merciless release from the tortuous round of pregnancies. So family planning becomes a humane issue. The mother's health and the welfare of her family will be all the better for smaller families and well-spaced children. But these considerations are hard to explain where the family pattern is traditionally large, where high infant mortality rates are expected (although less frequent with the spread of medical benefits) and where large families provide human insurance against death. It is difficult to convince peasants that fewer children increase the productivity per head of their fields; they think of children as more labour to reduce the tedious tasks of the rice field. And, of course, the bearing of sons is a matter of prestige to most peasant women.

MORAL AND RELIGIOUS OBJECTIONS

To tell men and women to produce fewer children is to trespass on their deepest personal relationship – the natural right to procreate. This presents a difficult moral problem but many questions have to be answered by those who resent this interference. Producing children does not end with the act of conception for their subsequent spiritual and material welfare is of the utmost concern. Is a child any better for being born into a miserable, disease-ridden existence than not being born at all? Is the world any better or worse for a bigger or smaller population? Is a large family, aching with hunger, any better than a smaller one, better fed? Is birth control less acceptable than race suicide through starvation? All men and women should be aware that such questions exist and recognize that their decisions to bring forth children are closely linked with a wider responsibility to the community.

No woman should be expected to produce as many children as is biologically possible. Most people will accept some form of limitation but argument is still rife on the methods allowed. In this respect religion plays an important rôle, for marriage has a religious basis in most societies. All the world's major religions, Christianity, Judaism, Islam, Buddhism, Confucianism and Hinduism allow birth control in the broad sense of restraint. But in the narrow sense of artificial contraception there is considerable controversy. The Roman Catholic Church is adamant that artificial control distorts the natural relationship between man and wife and is against the law of God. At the time of writing there is a very delicate argument in high Catholic circles in deciding whether the 'pill', which prevents ovulation, can be construed as a natural or artificial means of control. Certainly the use of the 'pill' may be a pointer to the type of control which could be accepted on moral and religious grounds in overpopulated regions, for both Hinduism and Buddhism allow natural methods.

CONCLUSION

The idea of tripling food production by the end of the century is a colossal requirement and the prospect is faced with a mixture of optimism and pessimism. The optimists point to the example of the last century in which food production not only matched but outstripped population growth. But these increased food supplies have been maldistributed throughout the world and we have witnessed the consequent effects of malnutrition. Moreover, the empty, pioneering grasslands are no longer free; those that remain are bound by the strings of national jealousy and prestige. And so the optimists put their faith virtually in a world nation. They recognize that the earth is capable of supporting over 6,000 million souls, but can do so by the turn of the century only if the governments of the world drop their national barriers and open their budgets to the world. The money spent on armaments, adequately and swiftly directed, could solve the problem. Despite the fine work of the United Nations, its various agencies and other government and voluntary organizations, however, there seems little hope that the world scene will be so miraculously changed. Daily the press and television inform us of new moves in the cold war. China looms as a menacing giant. The new, emergent nations squabble their way through adolescence. Capitalist countries pay for strategic vantage points. In all honesty, is there any prospect of this change to world co-operation taking place in the immediate future?

And so the pessimists take the stage. They see no immediate and real prospect of world-wide co-operation to increase food supplies to the required level and so they advocate swift action to counter the predicted population increase. Act now, they say, there is no gain in the world having a larger population. Restrict the supply of human beings quickly and the problem is solved. Time is increasing the odds against survival. Who can object to birth control replacing hunger, malnutrition and the disinclination to live?

It would be a wonderful testimony to the human race if the optimists could win but, with the world as we know it, the pessimists may have the only solution; otherwise, by the turn of the century, we may be entering the twilight of the golden age of the west on which the eastern sun is just rising.

TOPICS FOR DISCUSSION

1. Discuss the suggestion that education and birth control are the twin salvations of the world.

2. How far can governments interfere in the personal right to produce children?

3. Discuss the religious issues involved in birth control.

4. Outer space can wait its turn – the human being's my concern.

APPENDIX 1: THE VALIDITY OF POPULATION STATISTICS

The underdeveloped, explosive countries, the ones where the population problems are most acute, are the least reliable for statistical accuracy. In areas such as the mountain fastnesses of western China or the jungles of south-east Asia the registration of births and deaths is, for the most part, non-existent. With the absence of well-organized administrative machinery in such areas, illiteracy adding to the problem, the counting of heads is often haphazard and the charge of guess work is difficult to parry. Alfred Fabre-Luce, in *Men or Insects?* tells how, in 1930, he went to see the Chinese Foreign Minister who did not know, to within 100 millions, the population of his country. Apparently this vagueness was still evident in 1953 when a census, revealing 600 million Chinese, gave Mao Tse Tung a shock and prompted him to try to put a brake on this growth.

Even at home, the Registrar General would not claim that every single person was included in a census which is tightly administered. The 1961 Census for England and Wales was conducted in 1,315 census districts through the efforts of some 69,000 enumerators on one day. Such control would be impossible with the teeming masses of east and south-east Asia.

Most countries feed the United Nations Organization with population figures but its demographic year-book admits that only about half the actual births and deaths are registered (crude rates). Corrected rates can be devised by taking various sample surveys, sometimes self-contradictory because they are far from representative groups. Figures arrived at by these methods require constant qualification.

To offset these inaccuracies demographers base their estimates on the past experience of long-term growth trends from which, barring major catastrophes, *low*, *medium* and *high* assumptions are made. Models of the growth of population are taken on these assumptions related to the trend in birth and death rates for the area concerned, e.g. the assumption that the low death rates of industrialized countries will remain stable. There is no universally accepted formula for predicting population increases because the rates of, and conditions for, growth differ according to area. And so the total figures for the world's population are probably nearer the truth because they average the mistakes of high and low assumptions for areas where guesswork takes a hand.

Population statistics, therefore, particularly in underdeveloped areas, have to be treated with reserve; they are essential but, at best, approximate only. They cannot speak the whole truth but they are indispensable for the indication of trends. One thing is certain; experience of previous population figures has shown that past predictions have erred on the low side and, on this basis, the forecast that A.D. 2000 will see the 6,000 millions mark topped is likely to be true providing no major catastrophe, such as nuclear war, introduces a Malthusian check.

APPENDIX 2: ESTIMATED AND PROJECTED POPULATION

Estimated and Projected Population of the Continents and the World
A.D. 1900–2000* (Medium Assumption.)

Year	World	Africa	North America	Latin America	Asia	Europe incl. U.S.S.R.	Oceania
1900	1550	120	81	63	857	423	6
1925	1907	147	126	99	1020	505	10
1950	2497	199	168	163	1380	575	13
1975	3828	303	240	303	2210	751	21
2000	6267	517	312	592	3870	947	29

(Figures in Millions.)

* *Source:* U.N.O. *Population Studies No. 28 Future Growth of World Population.*

APPENDIX 3: WORLD[1] PRODUCTION OF MAIN AGRICULTURAL COMMODITIES

	Pre-war Average	Average 1948/9–1952/1	Average 1953/4–1957/8	Average 1958/9–1962/3	1962/3	1963/4 (Prelim)	Change in production 1962/3 to 1963/4
	Million metric Tons						Per cent
Wheat	144·7	155·4	187·9	222·6	235·6	220·8	−6
Barley	44·1	46·7	62·0	73·1	83·1	85·3	+3
Oats	64·0	60·6	59·2	54·1	48·5	47·0	−3
Maize	106·4	124·1	141·0	185·2	192·8	207·7	+8
Rice (milled)[2]	65·7	71·3	82·7	98·4	102·0	107·8	+6
Sugar	24·9	31·9	39·9	50·1	49·2	52·2	+6
Citrus Fruit	11·1	15·2	17·8	20·4	19·8	20·5	+4
Apples[3]	6·8	9·4	10·4	14·2	14·9	15·8	+6
Bananas	8·1	13·7	15·7	18·7	19·8	20·4	+3

Vegetable Oils & Oilseeds [4]	10·4	12·9	15·6	18·2	19·0	20·0	+5
Coffee	2·41	2·24	2·69	4·09	4·09	3·95	-3
Cocoa	0·74	0·76	0·81	1·10	1·17	1·24	+6
Tea	0·47	0·58	0·71	0·83	0·87	0·87	—
Wine	20·3	18·9	21·5	24·8	28·5	25·1	-20
Tobacco	2·29	2·71	3·15	3·32	3·48	3·63	+4
Cotton (lint)	5·99	6·78	7·99	8·78	9·63	9·85	+2
Jute [5]	1·51	2·00	1·94	2·59	2·60	2·86	+10
Wool (greasy)	1·61	1·79	2·12	2·46	2·51	2·55	+2
Rubber (natural)	1·00	1·74	1·89	2·06	2·14	2·09	-2
Milk	221·0	261·3	301·5	344·0	354·7	350·9	-1
Meat [6]	29·4	36·6	45·0	51·6	54·9	56·5	+3
Eggs	6·32	8·77	10·64	12·58	13·3	13·4	+1

Source: United Nations F.A.O. The State of Food & Agriculture 1964.
[1] Excluding Mainland China. [2] Paddy converted at 65 per cent. [3] Excluding U.S.S.R. [4] Oil equivalent. [5] Including allied fibres. [6] Beef and veal, mutton and lamb, pig meat.

APPENDIX 4: SOME TERMS EXPLAINED

Birth rate usually implies the crude birth rate which is the number of live births in each year for each thousand of the population.

Cultivated land is the sown area, fallow or temporary pastures, but usually excludes permanent pastures.

Death rate is the crude death rate which is the number of deaths in each year for each thousand of the population.

Decade: A period of ten years.

Demography is the study of population statistics.

Fertility rate is the extent to which women actually bear children.

Generation is the average time taken for children to become parents – usually twenty-five to thirty years.

Life expectancy: The number of years a person can expect to live, *on the average,* from birth.

Mortality: The frequency of deaths in any group of people.

Natural increase: The actual difference between the number of births and the number of deaths in any group of people.

Overpopulation: The state in which too many people crowd into a given land area and are unable to live efficiently and decently.

Population density is the ratio of population to any given land area.

Population estimates: Population figures given at the mid-year point.

Population increase is the natural increase plus or minus the difference between emigrants and immigrants.

Population pressure is the extent to which population can be supported by the existing economic resources of a given land area.

Rate of natural increase is the difference between the birth rate and death rate of a country or area.

Resources are the agricultural, mineral and industrial potential, together with manpower, on which a country can rely for its economic security.

Underdeveloped country. A country which has not developed, by Western standards, its agricultural and/or industrial resources to the full. Such countries have low standards of living.